Digital Marketing Trends and Prospects

Develop an Effective Digital Marketing
Strategy with SEO, SEM, PPC,
Digital Display Ads and
Email Marketing Techniques

Dr. Shakti Kundu

www.bpbonline.com

FIRST EDITION 2021

Copyright © BPB Publications, India

ISBN: 978-93-89898-583

Distributors:

BPB PUBLICATIONS
20, Ansari Road, Darya Ganj
New Delhi-110002
Ph: 23254990/23254991

DECCAN AGENCIES
4-3-329, Bank Street,
Hyderabad-500195
Ph: 24756967/24756400

MICRO MEDIA
Shop No. 5, Mahendra Chambers,
150 DN Rd. Next to Capital Cinema,
V.T. (C.S.T.) Station, MUMBAI-400 001
Ph: 22078296/22078297

BPB BOOK CENTRE
376 Old Lajpat Rai Market,
Delhi-110006
Ph: 23861747

To View Complete
BPB Publications Catalogue
Scan the QR Code:

Published by Manish Jain for BPB Publications, 20 Ansari Road, Darya Ganj, New Delhi-110002 and Printed by him at Repro India Ltd, Mumbai

Dedicated to

Every challenging work needs self efforts as well as the guidance of elders, especially those who are very close to our heart.

I dedicate my humble efforts to my sweet and loving father and mother (Shri. Shamsher Kundu and Smt. Anupama Kundu). Their affection, love, encouragement, and prayers of day and night enabled me to get such success and honor.

THANK YOU

About the Author

 **Dr. Shakti Kundu** is working as an Associate Professor in the Faculty of Engineering and Computing Sciences at Teerthanker Mahaveer University (TMU), Moradabad, Uttar Pradesh, India. His current research interests are Digital Marketing, Software Engineering, Information Security, Web Data Mining, and Intelligent Systems. He brings to his classes over 13 years of teaching experience. He has worked with various reputed universities and holds administrate experience as well. He has chaired and delivered various technical sessions at the national and international levels and has published more than 41 research papers in reputed journals and conferences, which are indexed in various international databases. Dr. Kundu has edited two books and authored ten book chapters in the field of Software Engineering and Digital Marketing with national and international publishers. Moreover, he has published two patents in the field of Artificial Intelligence, Machine Learning and Deep Learning. He is a life member of CSI, ISTE, IAENG, AIRCC, and IAEME.

About the Reviewers

◆ **Harjinder Singh** is working as an Assistant Professor in the Faculty of Engineering and Computing Sciences at Teerthanker Mahaveer University, Moradabad, Uttar Pradesh, India. He completed his MCA from the Uttar Pradesh Technical University, Lucknow. The project work during his internship was on **"Satellite Image Processing and Contextual Entropy Based Fuzzy Classifier Tool"** at the Indian Institute of Remote Sensing, Dehradun. He worked with WIPRO Technologies, Pune for more than three years as a project engineer for **VANTIV**, one of the reputed card payment industries of America. He has taught subjects like Android, Core Java, and Python. Mr. Harjinder Singh has supervised many UG and PG students for their project works. He brings to his classes the combination of the IT industry and academia exposure.

LinkedIn profile:

https://www.linkedin.com/in/harjinder-singh-3ba8311b2

◆ **Narender Singh** did his M.C.A. from Lovely Professional University in Jalandhar, Punjab, India. He has qualified UGC NET, HTET national level exams. He has published several research articles in various international journals. His current research interests are Data Science, Software Engineering, and Information Security. He has two years of teaching experience.

Acknowledgement

There are a few people I want to thank for the continued support they have given me during the writing of this book. First and foremost, I would like to thank my parents, wife, and son Shaurya for putting up with me when I was spending many weekends and evenings on writing. I could have never completed this book without their support.

This book would not have happened if I did not have the support of my colleague(s) and students. My gratitude goes to Prof. R. K. Dwivedi, Director, FOECS/TMU for providing valuable insights into some of the new features and allowing me to have access to the impressive digital multimedia and animation lab at Teerthanker Mahaveer University, Moradabad, Uttar Pradesh, India.

Finally, I would like to thank BPB Publications for giving me this opportunity to write my first book for them.

Preface

Digital marketing can be called as the process of promoting brands or products using electronic media. It is the medium which fulfils the demand, want, or need of both entities, that is, the users as well as the marketers. It publicizes the content on the digital platforms with the support of its elements for various domains such as B2B, B2C, and NPF marketing.

SEO stands for search engine optimization. It is the process or technique of gaining traffic, visibility, and rank on search engines through both paid and unpaid efforts. SEO is a set of rules for optimizing your website for search engines and to improve your search engine rankings. The search engine optimization strategy helps in making your website active.

E-mail marketing is a precious and reasonable way for business owners to promote their brand, products, and services. It allows them to approach customers and build a solid relationship with them. It involves using e-mail to give promotion to products and services with the purpose of enhancing a relationship with present as well as new customers. This strategy helps in achieving market targets.

Social media marketing is now a proven way for companies to reach new customers, interact with old customers, and encourage the tone, mission, or culture. It helps in exploring your business in the digital world with the directions of setting up a business page on social media platforms with the support of techniques, tools, and strategies. With the inclusion of interactive media content and landing pages, social media marketing fulfils the requirements of reaching potential users in an easy manner.

Mobile marketing is used to approach potential customers through multi-channel promotion of products and services. Marketers publicize their brand and goods with extensive use of mobile gadgets. They reach to the widest range of audiences with varying options for mobiles such as mobile apps, e-mail, in-app advertising, and so on. It helps in enhancing the growth of your business in the digital platform. It highlights your brand and products for promotion through mobile features and technology.

The primary goal of this book is to provide the information and skills that are necessary for end users as well as marketers to understand the real scenario of digital marketing. This book contains real-time examples that will help you in remembering, analyzing, applying and creating the various trends and prospects of digital marketing.

This book is composed of an introduction and 5 chapters, each of which consist of conclusions at the end. The conclusions present the original contributions of the author and point out the directions for the next chapter. Over the five chapters in this book, you will learn the following:

Chapter 1 - Introduction to Digital Marketing comprises of the basic concepts of marketing and their importance. In addition, various elements of marketing are highlighted with relevant examples. Lastly, the benefits and opportunities of digital marketing and its usage in business to business (B2B), business to consumer (B2C), and not for profit (NFP) marketing are discussed.

Chapter 2 - Search Engine Optimization (SEO): The core of digital marketing contains an overview of the important theoretical concepts and technological aspects of search engine optimization. It summarizes the importance of SEO, search results, and positioning. Moreover, a detailed description of on-page and off-page optimization, backlinks, internal and external links, rankings, SEO site map, and how to proceed with steps for B2B SEO and B2C SEO are expressed.

Chapter 3 - E-mail Marketing and Digital Display Advertising highlights the description related to the elements, list, structure, and delivery of an e-mail. Furthermore, a detailed discussion is done on gathering offline and online data for e-mail marketing. To evaluate the success of the campaign, the concept of A/B testing and its implementation in e-mail marketing is summarized. Besides these, the concepts, benefits, and challenges of digital display advertising are conveyed.

Chapter 4 - Social Media Marketing describes the key impact of social media on search engine optimization based on key metrics like CPC, PPC, CPM, CTR, and CPA which take into account the different aspects of social marketing and its behavior. This chapter defines the basic concepts of user-generated content, multimedia video, multimedia audio, and multimedia images.

Chapter 5 - Mobile Marketing and Web Analytics contains the presentation of mobile apps and its comparison with widgets. An overview related to B2B and B2C mobile marketing is discussed. A part of this chapter highlights the feasibility of providing relevant information related to user access through web analytics tools and its process. Furthermore, how to generate traffic and behavior report is an informative section and the concluding one.

This book will give you in-depth knowledge of digital marketing by learning about many real-life examples in the scenario of digital marketing based on the latest versions of marketing strategies and techniques.

Downloading the coloured images:

Please follow the link to download the
Coloured Images of the book:

https://rebrand.ly/ff934

Errata

We take immense pride in our work at BPB Publications and follow best practices to ensure the accuracy of our content to provide with an indulging reading experience to our subscribers. Our readers are our mirrors, and we use their inputs to reflect and improve upon human errors, if any, that may have occurred during the publishing processes involved. To let us maintain the quality and help us reach out to any readers who might be having difficulties due to any unforeseen errors, please write to us at :

errata@bpbonline.com

Your support, suggestions and feedbacks are highly appreciated by the BPB Publications' Family.

Did you know that BPB offers eBook versions of every book published, with PDF and ePub files available? You can upgrade to the eBook version at www.bpbonline.com and as a print book customer, you are entitled to a discount on the eBook copy. Get in touch with us at :

business@bpbonline.com for more details.

At **www.bpbonline.com**, you can also read a collection of free technical articles, sign up for a range of free newsletters, and receive exclusive discounts and offers on BPB books and eBooks.

BPB is searching for authors like you

If you're interested in becoming an author for BPB, please visit **www.bpbonline.com** and apply today. We have worked with thousands of developers and tech professionals, just like you, to help them share their insight with the global tech community. You can make a general application, apply for a specific hot topic that we are recruiting an author for, or submit your own idea.

The code bundle for the book is also hosted on GitHub at **https://github.com/bpbpublications/Digital-Marketing-Trends-and-Prospects**. In case there's an update to the code, it will be updated on the existing GitHub repository.

We also have other code bundles from our rich catalog of books and videos available at **https://github.com/bpbpublications**. Check them out!

PIRACY

If you come across any illegal copies of our works in any form on the internet, we would be grateful if you would provide us with the location address or website name. Please contact us at :

business@bpbonline.com with a link to the material.

If you are interested in becoming an author

If there is a topic that you have expertise in, and you are interested in either writing or contributing to a book, please visit **www.bpbonline.com**.

REVIEWS

Please leave a review. Once you have read and used this book, why not leave a review on the site that you purchased it from? Potential readers can then see and use your unbiased opinion to make purchase decisions, we at BPB can understand what you think about our products, and our authors can see your feedback on their book. Thank you!

For more information about BPB, please visit **www.bpbonline.com**.

Table of Contents

CHAPTER 1
Introduction to Digital Marketing

Digital marketing can be called as the process of promoting brands or products using electronic media. So what is the difference between digital marketing and traditional marketing? What is the current scenario of digital marketing? You will find the answer to these questions in this chapter and the subsequent ones. So let's get started!

Structure

In this chapter, we will cover the following topics:

Objective

After studying this chapter, you should be able to:

- Understand the importance and scope of marketing
- Understand the concept of digital marketing
- Understand the benefits and opportunities of digital marketing

1.1 Introduction to marketing

Marketing is an approach of business functionalities that includes various phases engaged in creating, analyzing, managing, delivering products, and the related services. It also focuses on maintaining customer relationships, resulting in mutual benefits of customers and the stakeholders.

It is the technique of choosing the market targets with criteria of market analysis and segmentation. Market analysis is done based on the buying behavioral characteristics of the user. The basic objective of this place is to provide the best customer value.

However, the marketing agenda is considered to be successful only when the business exists as a whole, which is followed by an organization's vision, mission, tasks, and the ability to adopt technology as per current the demand and scenario.

It can also be considered as a matter of intelligent perspective because it is observed as an indicator of an organization's success. For example, Patanjali, Dabur, and Wipro must rely on marketing strategies to grow and keep their customer strength and its base.

1.2 Types of marketing

The types of marketing that are functioning in the real-world are as follows:

- **Traditional marketing:** To capture the market targets, it covers varying offline steps such as door-to-door selling, print advertisement, radio, television direct mails, and so on.

- **Digital marketing:** It benefits from the usage of the internet to arrive at its respective markets via social media channels, e-mails, websites, video sites, mobile apps, and online feedback forms.

- **Social media marketing:** It performs well when used in combination with other marketing strategies. It is a popular way of doing business and connects with audiences in an effective manner. It is also considered a helpful brand builder and market research tool.

- **Mobile marketing:** It is considered as one of the important marketing approaches in today's framework. It helps customers in getting their information in one click.

1.3 Evolution of marketing concepts

Here is a brief overview of the evolution of marketing concepts:

a) **Production concept:** This concept focuses more on the need for the product. Its aim is to fulfil the expectation of the user in terms of product availability at affordable prices. Moreover, the focus is on lowering the cost and increasing the mass distribution.

b) **Product concept:** This approach gives attention to the user's expectations towards their desired products. It is assumed in product concept criteria that users are more likely to be loyal once the product meets all their requirements. This thought comes up with business drivers to offer better, highly fulfilling, unique, and rich features based products.

   c) **Selling concept:** This concept concentrates on selling the products through active promotion. The belief behind this concept is that customers will respond only when the product is pushed. The strategy is to sell the product however it is produced rather than to create a product that meets the user needs.

   d) **Marketing concept:** This approach focuses on the buyer rather than the seller. It is different from the earlier stated marketing concepts because it believes in pull marketing. This marketing concept is buyer-oriented as it gives credit to the user by creating brand loyalty. Moreover, its objective is to give attention to the needs, wants, and desires of the user.

1.4 Importance and scope of marketing

The scope of marketing is very wide as it covers all the activities from the onception of ideas to realization. Generally, the users' expectation are towards their wants and needs. Products are created to satisfy the user's requirements in terms of wants. So, a discussion is required to determine the users' needs and wants. Some of the most important scopes of marketing are as follows:

1) Goods

Goods are one of the important aspects of any country and are as per its desires and needs. Physical goods are considered to be a vital section of production and marketing efforts. For example, billions of food products, millions of vehicles, and electronic appliances are marketed by various companies.

2) Services

Services are directly or indirectly proportional to goods or products. The main goal of any successful organization is to satisfy the users with its goods and services. To increase the sales and maintain faith with the users, it is necessary to keep services as one of the important elements of marketing in an active mode. For example, a company offering home appliances to its users with a mix of goods and services.

3) Events

Events are one of the important elements of the scope of marketing. There are various moments that capture the scenario of events such as award shows, company anniversaries, trade shows, health shows, awareness camps, and so on. For example, global sporting events such as the commonwealth games are promoted energetically to both companies and fans.

4) **Experiences**

Experiences help in making an impact on the user's mind with theor characteristics or features. For example, a residential township offers a clubhouse, swimming pool, sports court, and other services in the form of experiences to its customers. In short, marketers share experiences by offering a mix of both goods and services. A good is popularized not only by its features but also by sharing its unique and valuable experience to customers.

5) **Persons**

Persons are becoming the popular scope of marketing from the last decade. Famous personalities such as sportspersons, film stars, and TV stars have their own personal managers and marketing agents. These personal managers are further tied-up with public relations marketing agencies to better publicize or highlight the person's personality in the market.

6) **Places**

Places have helped in raising the scope of marketing for so many decades. In fact, it is one of the important elements of marketing. In the current situation, cities, states, and countries are also marketing their places as hot spots to increase the revenue bar of tourism. For example, places like temples, malls, exhibition grounds, stadiums, etc. are becoming important assets in the form of places for marketing purposes. These types of hot spots are effectively promoted by the tourism ministry or industries in both local as well as global regions.

7) **Properties**

Properties are playing a major role in the scope of marketing. With the decent amount of development in the past few decades, people make investments in properties through their savings and other financial supports. Properties are bought and sold through marketing. The demand and supply of properties is making awareness among the public through marketing strategies. These approaches help in highlighting the scope of properties in the real world. Any type of category of properties needs to build trust and confidence at higher levels through the various aspects of marketing.

8)   Organizations

To raise an organization to a new height of success, its image and reputation actually matter a lot. Organizations work hard day and night to build a positive image in the minds of the tier target users. The public relations domain does a lot of exercise in marketing an organization's image with a positive impact. The organization's fruitful image helps in the smooth launching of their new and proposed products. In addition, their goodwill provides support in representing their strong and effective image in the real world.

9)   Information

Information is one of the strongest mediums of marketing. Due to increased literacy rate and awareness level, information is becoming an important tool for marketing. Also, in the digital era and the media revolution, the need and demand for information is growing very rapidly moment by moment. Information can also be produced and marketed as a product. Educational institutions, government agencies, research and development, and non-governmental organizations are various examples of the origination of the information.

10)   Idea

Products and services are two phases of the coin. Here, coin is resembling an example of the marketing scenario. These products and services are considered as two important pillars of the marketing platforms which help in sharing some idea or benefit. For example, Dettol promotes its various products with the tag line "Be 100% Sure." This is one of the cases of the idea that social marketers generally follow in wide promotions and awareness.

1.5 Elements of marketing

The concept of marketing consists of various elements such as needs, wants, marketing offers, consumer value and satisfaction, markets, marketers, and prospects. Each element of marketing highlights its meaning, role, and application in the functioning environment.

1.5.1 Needs

Needs are the passions or wishes that re categorized on the basis of different circumstances such as:

Psychological needs: This type of need belongs to fundamental or essential needs. For example, food, shelter, clothing, and education are cases of psychological needs.

Security needs: This category of needs occurs in a human being's life in various instances either naturally or artificially. Every human being expects protection from any loss or failure because he or she wants risk-free living.

Esteem needs: This kind of need involves the appreciation or respect that people generally like to achieve. But to achieve such a case of need, people have to go through the phases of competition.

Actualization needs: This class of needs focuses on self-actualization needs. For instance, if one eats ordinary rice, then another is thinking of basmati rice; if one has a Tata Nano car, then another has opinion on a Mercedes car. So, actualization highlights the natural phenomenon of life where each human being desires to go ahead in each phase of life.

1.5.2 Wants

Want is one of the vital elements of marketing. The 'Wants' terminology is used in the concept of marketing which means need plus capacity to pay. For example, if in the event of a food festival, you are offered free banana shake to taste with no limit, then in that case, there is a high probability that you may want more than one glass of banana shake to drink. On the other side, if that banana shake is an offer on a paid basis, then you may wonder whether to order it or not. That means that a want is something that is chosen from needs.

Generally, needs may be essential or basic needs such as food, shelter, and so on. But wants discuss your need and potential to pay. For example, a rich person has a demand for a luxury car, but it is only wanted by a middle-class person and a mere need for economically weaker section person.

There is always a variation in the degree of wants and needs. If we think from the perspective of a human being's nature, then for wants, a person's approach is infinite or uncountable but in the case of needs, a person's direction is finite or countable.

1.5.3 Marketing offers

Marketers and organizations involved in marketing provide various offers as per the need of the user. A marketing offer means a presentation of products that meets the requirement of consumers in varying parameters such as quality, quantity, price, validity, and so on. In addition, the consumer looks for additional parameters of the product wherein whether it falls in the category of a tangible product or intangible product.

A tangible product is one that is visible, tested, and self-realized by the senses whereas an intangible product is one that is invisible, not portable, and we get to know the exact details of the product at the point of the receiving time and place. Further, the products may be broadly categorized as manufacturing goods and produced goods.

Manufactured goods refer to those things that can be broadly categorized into two categories, namely durable and non-durable. These goods are built up with the support of individuals and automation. For instance, electronic appliances are durable things and eatable items are non-durable things.

In produced goods, nature and technology play an important role in the production. For example, milk, eggs, vegetables, fruits, ghee, chicken, mutton, beef, and honey are produced goods.

Each organization has a market offer consisting of a mixed package of products and services. This marketing offer further includes offers to customers through two domains, that is, the product line and the service line. Normally, the customer initially chooses the product line and then the service line.

Companies present their product portfolio which helps the consumer in making the decision of selecting the product during the phase of the product line. Afterwards, they look for services associated with the respective product during the phase of the service line.

The main objective of marketing offers is to satisfy the consumer requirement with the maximum number of benefits at the minimum price.

1.5.4 Consumer value and satisfaction

The consumer assumes product acceptability on the basis of two parameters: value and satisfaction. Consumers evolve a level of satisfaction on the basis of the scope of the product and its associated services.

In short, a consumer value is examined by the degree of satisfaction. If the degree of satisfaction is low, it means a product is of low value and if the degree of satisfaction is high, it indicates that a product is of high value to the consumer.

Satisfaction is one of the parameters that are considered from the producer and consumer's perspective. In fact, satisfaction cannot be measured as it cannot be quantified. The role of cost helps in justifying the degree of satisfaction. For example, if an item is available free of cost or at much-discounted rates, then the user will grab that offer; otherwise, if a similar item is available at a high cost, then the user will disallow that item.

The bottom line is that satisfaction is measured as per the consumer's need or want. For instance, a father is interested in buying a luxury car as he thinks it is the right age and also has the capacity to buy it. On the other hand, his son is thinking of pursuing higher studies in abroad. Now, in such a circumstance, both the car and the course are costly and in the interests of both to proceed. But the father can go ahead with either one of the options. Now in such a situation, the father sacrifices his idea of buying a car and moves ahead in support of his son's higher education that has the high scope of job opportunities with a handsome pay package once he becomes a post-graduate.

Here, one can define 'cost' to the consumer as the monetary value of what is bought. In fact, it is a major issue under consideration in marketing because it means a sacrifice of some alternative or the other on the part of the consumer.

1.5.5 Markets

A market is a platform where two entities come together in person and do the relevant marketing. The two entities are buyers and sellers. It is the medium where buyers and sellers contact each other with detailed information related to the marketing procedure. The information includes what the sellers have to offer and what the buyers are ready to buy.

It is the process where the negotiation mechanism takes place related to the price fixation on the basis of mutual benefits of buyers as well as sellers.

Moreover, three cases are held during the negotiation procedure. Either the deal is accepted, rejected, or kept on hold by the buyer and seller. If both the buyer and seller agree with each other as per the stated information, then it is accepted. If they do not agree, then the deal rejected, and there is no conclusion, then it is kept on hold (which means that it can be considered for discussion in the near future).

1.5.6 Marketer and prospects

A marketer is a medium that provides a marketing platform. In this platform, he highlights his own portfolio and range of goods that are available for sale. Marketers, with their skill set, establish a marketing platform, time ownership, and awareness campaign program.

Marketers do not produce but buy from producers and sell to consumers for further processing and sale.

All the related functioning of marketers is based on prospects. The existence of marketers is dependent on the availability of prospects, that is, a marketer's presence is directly proportional to prospects. If nobody will be available to buy the goods and services, then there will be no scope of existence for marketers.

That's why prospects are consumers and they are in the hot seat of the framework of the marketing system. Additionally, the prospect is an organization or individual who has the capacity to buy and pay for the goods and their related services. The crux of the discussion is that marketers and prospects are proportional to each other. If any one side of the entity is missing, then the respective task will not proceed.

1.6 Marketing vs. sales

Marketing is the concept whose aim is to detect or find the needs of human beings and further satisfy the user on the basis of their needs and profitability requirements. On the other hand, the responsibility of sales is to convince customers to make the purchase of goods or services offered by the company.

Table 1.1 discusses the comparison between marketing and sales with the help of various parameters such as definition, approach, focus, process, scope, horizon, strategy, priority, and identity.

	Marketing	Sales
Definition	Marketing is an organized way that is used to create a common platform and controls business activities to bring together buyers and sellers.	Sale is a transaction activity that is applicable between two entities where the buyer receives goods, services, or assets in exchange for money.
Approach	Marketing performs a wider range of activities to sell goods. It regulates needs and makes a strategy to meet those needs for a long-term relationship.	Sales matches the customer demand with the products that the company presently offers.
Focus	Marketing's focus is to promote the price of products and services and also to meet the customer's wants and needs through products or services that the company can offer.	It focuses on making the sales volume.
Process	Marketing performs and looks over varying processes such as analysis of market, distribution channels, competitive products and services, pricing strategies, sales tracking, and market share analysis.	Sales prefers to do its process on one-to-one basis.
Scope	The scope of marketing includes market research, advertising, sales, public relations, and customer service and satisfaction.	Sales convinces the customers to purchase the product to meet their needs.
Horizon	Long-term	Short-term
Strategy	Pull	Push
Priority	Marketing shows how to reach to the customers and build long-lasting relationships.	Selling is the ultimate result of marketing.
Identity	Marketing's objective is to build the brand identity so that it gets easily linked with the customer's needs.	There is no reach of brand identity. It is simply the ability to meet a need at the right time.

Table 1.1: Comparison between marketing and sales

1.7 Introduction to digital marketing

Digital marketing may be defined as the method of promoting products or brands through online platforms. It primarily takes place on the internet.

Traditional marketing performs its activities through the offline mode. It has limited ability to reach customers.

Digital marketing is the term used for the targeted, measurable, and interactive marketing of products or services using digital technologies to reach the viewers, turn them into customers, and retain them.

The traditional manner of marketing involved businesses to advertise their products or services in print media, radio and television commercials, business cards, and in many other similar ways where the internet or social media websites were not employed for advertising.

Table 1.2 discusses the comparison between traditional marketing and digital marketing.

Digital marketing	Traditional marketing
Conversation is two-way.	Conversation is one-way.
Consumers are free to interact or share suggestions regarding products and services.	Company communicates about its products and services to audiences.
Channel of correspondence is online mode.	Channel of correspondence is offline mode.
It is a less time-consuming technique.	It is a more time-consuming method.
Websites, e-mail, and social media channels are examples of digital marketing.	Letters, phone calls, and billboards are examples of traditional marketing.
Demonstration is much easier with the support of digital technologies.	More effort is required for traditional campaigning such as creation, publishing, displaying, etc.

Its reach to target audience is the widest, that is, at the global level.	Its reach to target audience is minimal, that is, at the local level.
It is easier to measure the impact of demonstration.	It is difficult to measure the effectiveness of a campaign.

Table 1.2: Comparisons between traditional marketing and digital marketing

1.8 Benefits and opportunities for digital marketing

The benefits of digital marketing include:

- **Wider reach:** Digital marketing has a wider reach, that is, globally through its digital support such as websites, e-mail, blogs, and many other digital media.

- **Minimal cost:** The address and demonstration of digital marketing activities is always at a minimal cost in comparison to the traditional approaches.

- **Easily traceable and measurable:** It is easier to measure and trace the effect of a digital campaign. With the help of digital tools such as web analytics, you may get the relevant information regarding the activities of users towards your website. The behaviour of users includes information like the number of hits, files and page visits, and so on. Additionally, digital tools help in taking decision-making steps towards the business on the basis of the generated analytical report.

- **Integration:** Digital marketing features include the concept of integration. In this approach, the user profile is linked with the respective website. Due to this integration, communication between the buyer and seller become more effective. This two-way technique helps the marketer in sharing various offers and greetings from time to time. In short, the more the accessibility of users; the more will be productive marketing.

- **Accountability:** Digital marketing believes in openness. To maintain the scenario of accountability, it is necessary to get involved with users and manage the professional relationship with ease on the social media platforms.

- **Social currency:** By organizing various digital campaigns with rich content, it becomes easier to get connected with audiences. With this activity, there is a high probability of gaining social currency which is further passed from user to user and takes the form of viral mode.

- **Improved conversion rates:** Through the website, e-mail, and other digital modes, there is a high probability to catch customers which are merely a few clicks away from your purchasing zone. So, the improvisation of the conversion rate is much higher in the digital marketing platform.

1.9 Inbound and outbound marketing

Inbound marketing is one of the ways of marketing in which your ads will appear only when people search for the products or services you offer. It includes the concept of paid search advertising.

Outbound marketing is another medium of marketing that finds customers, initiates conversation, and sends information in the form of a message to people regardless of their interest.

Table 1.3 discusses the comparison between inbound and outbound marketing.

Inbound	Outbound
Pulls in interested readers.	Pushes at everybody regardless of interest.
Written for the consumer's needs.	Written for the product's needs.
Interactive and fluid.	Fixed and one-way.
Draws in customers.	Seeks out customers.
Part of content consumption.	Disrupts content consumption.
Inbound marketing includes blogs, social media channels, opt-in emails, and search.	Outbound marketing includes display ads, billboards, telemarketer scripts, magazines, and TV ads.

Table 1.3: Comparisons between Inbound and Outbound

1.10 Content marketing

Content marketing refers to the target online audience. It is a kind of marketing that focuses on making, printing, and sharing content for online users.

It is a form of marketing that does not directly promote a brand or item but its purpose is to energize interest in the user's mind through the products or services. It consists of the creation and distribution of information to its online users through videos, blogs, and social media posts. It is often used by businesses to:

- Attract attention and generate leads
- Expand their customer base
- Generate or increase online sales
- Increase brand awareness or credibility
- Engage an online community of users

Content marketing helps organizations in justifying brand loyalty. Additionally, it provides relevant information to consumers and creates an eagerness to purchase the product and its related services from the organization in the future. It also attracts prospects and transforms the prospects into users by creating and distributing valuable free content. This is a relatively new type of marketing that does not include the method of direct sales. Instead, it builds bonds and faith with the targeted online audience.

Unlike other forms of online marketing, content marketing relies on meeting and estimating the needs of an existing or new customer through priceless or meaningful information.

1.11 Understanding traffic

Traffic in an online platform is measured through various parameters or activities that actually happens in websites through web users. This type of movement is also known as web traffic. It is calculated by the number of visits, hits, and time spent.

Web traffic does not include the web data generated by software robots or bots. Instead, it highlights the amount of data sent and received by web users to a website. Since the last two decades, the internet traffic has increased very rapidly in which the largest portion of web traffic data is generated through websites. This is monitored by the number of hits, visitors, and number of pages visited. The web traffic movement is traced by weblog analyzer tools. These tools capture the on-going site activities such as which parts or pages of their site are popular. Also, which page is viewed mostly by web users and in what duration. There are various ways to monitor web traffic and gathering of web data helps a lot in understanding traffic which further assists or guides in structuring the web sites, handling security problems, and suggesting a proper bandwidth for the smooth functioning of thr sites.

There is another aspect of web traffic. Some organizations offer schemes, for example, they would pay for screen space on the site if the number of web visitors will reach their expected limit. To make themselves popular on sites, some sites often aim to increase their web traffic through the involvement of search engine optimization. This approach is being is followed by sites that result in an increase in web traffic.

1.12 Understanding leads

Leads generation is one of the methods which falls under the category of advertising. In marketing terminology, it is the initiative of user inquiry or interest related to the product or services offered by an organization or company. It may also include sources such as referrals from existing users which are non-paid.

Leads can be created for varying purposes like list building, sales leads, and so on. The term sales lead states that it consists of information related to interested users or clients who show curiosity in the company's product or service and further want to remain in the loop of things while sharing their contact details.

There are various sources or origins for lead generation. For example, personal referrals, advertisements, events, internet, and telephone calls either by the company or telemarketers. A recent study explored some interesting facts about lead generation. From the survey, we came to know that 89% of respondents prefer e-mail citation as the most preferred approach for generating leads. Another fact that came into knowledge was that search engines, web referrals, and direct traffic are considered to be the topmost used social media channels for lead generation activities, resulting in the generation of 93% of leads.

The term pipeline marketing refers to the combination of tasks done for the fulfilment of the common goal of marketing. Lead generation is regularly tied up with lead management under the phenomenon of pipeline marketing to move leads through the purchase pathway.

A lead is allotted to an individual, for example, a salesperson, or a counselor to follow up. Once the respective individual reviews and qualifies it to potential business, the lead gets transformed as an opportunity for further business activities which undergoes multiple stages of the sales process before the deal is won.

There are three types of leads in the lead generation market:

- **Sales leads:** Sales lead refers to the information that identifies an entity as a potential buyer of the products and services. Here, the entity can be a person, company, or business about which the information is to be stored and further used for business activities. Through advertising, trade shows, and other marketing efforts, companies can gain access to sales leads.

- **Marketing leads:** Marketing leads is one of the concepts of lead generation that refers to a technique where the interest of the potential customer is transformed to turn them into buyers. Sales leads can be resold to many advertisers whereas marketing leads can be sold only once. Its main objective is to indicate interest about what the brand has to offer based on marketing efforts and further get connected to potential buyers.

- **Investor lead:** Investor lead is initiated by an investor who plays the role of a lead investor. A small-medium enterprise generally takes the help of a lead investor for their business to have financial support for their start-up. A lead investor is the first person who invests in the proposed start-up and remains in the process of starting up before, during, and even after a fundraiser moment. As an investor, the lead investor contributes towards the growth of the business with his dedication and passionate investment skills.

1.13 Digital marketing use in business-to-business, business-to-consumer, and not-for-profit marketing

The usage of digital marketing in various domains of marketing helps in understanding the overall behavioral characteristics of marketing in the digital era.

Business-to-business (B2B)

Business-to-business marketing or B2B marketing refers to the sale of one company's product or services to another company. The B2B marketing technique believes in the same basic principles as consumer marketing but is executed in a different way.

Consumers choose products on various factors such as price, quantity, popularity, status, and other emotional triggers but B2B buyers make decisions on two major potentials: profit and price.

B2B marketing has established new relationships through social media to speed up the process of conversation between businesses. As per the recent study, the fact came into the picture that businesses are more likely to buy from companies that they can track through social media.

B2B companies start representing themselves as tech-savvy companies because this transformed and innovative approach helps them in reaching their market targets with added-on advantage. For example, the CISCO system incorporation, a leading seller of networking systems, launched its new product exclusively on social media advertising. This initiative helped the company in saving a huge amount of money that they had planned earlier through normal launch activity.

B2B marketers generally focus on major classifications like brokers, wholesalers, hospitals, schools, construction companies, and government agencies. A B2B marketer can successfully place their products or services into the right hands by positioning their offering in an exciting manner, by understanding the customer's needs, and proposing the right solutions to the customers.

Business-to-consumer (B2C)

Business-to-consumer marketing or B2C marketing refers to the method in which a company promotes its product and services to individual people. It is a fact that no B2C company can survive without doing some kind of marketing. B2C marketing makes, publishes, distributes various advertisements, and further sell products to customers that are useful in their everyday lives.

The impulse buying nature of consumer makes them to do the purchasing of products in minimal time and with maximum discounts. Consumers expect to receive some offers, benefits, or discounts from their purchase, but they generally do not put on the scale of the financial risks as heavily as businesses do.

Efficient or functional B2C marketers very well know about the impulse behavior of consumers. For this, they brush up campaigns that connect with the consumer's mindset. Additionally, B2C marketers work to convert shoppers to buyers as soon as possible through discount offers, advertisements, direct and indirect marketing strategies.

Those selling consumer-based products typically engage in some form of B2C marketing. For example, restaurants may promote their dishes or food with additional services like food of the day, food discounts, their environment, and reputation. Clothing and make-up companies do much of their marketing through the concept of fashion which can be changed whenever there is a new product to sell. Car companies promote their existing or newly launched car models through road trips, test drives, festival offers, or discounts. Food companies selling in grocery stores promote their items via advertisements, variety of items availability, freshness, product packaging, and delivery.

Not-for-Profit (NFP) marketing

Not-for-profit marketing or NFP marketing refers to the approach of marketing which is done through various mediums such as e-mail marketing, social media, content marketing, regular engagement with supporters, websites, and so on. Here are a few basics that organizations generally follow:

- **E-mail marketing:** E-mail is one of the best mediums to reach users or potential customers. It is one of the least expensive and most effective ways of not-for-profit marketing. Through e-mail, we can keep our supporters up to date on recent developments, but it is important that your e-mail content and its presentation should be fruitful and attractive. An e-mail that contains bulky paragraph-based text and dull images is more likely to be painful to potential users rather than any help. The best approach is to send a precise, summarized, formatted, and well-structured e-mail with a minimum frequency of twice a month. With this best practice, the motive to connect to the potential users will be achieved with high impact.

- **Social media:** The presence of social media has made communication more effective in the global world. It is one of the effective tools of not-for-profit marketing. Through various social media platforms like Facebook, Twitter, LinkedIn, it becomes easier to share all sorts of effective campaign information to a wider audience. With few lines of code, you can add social media sharing buttons to your websites and e-mails. It helps in reaching and connecting from wider to widest audiences.

- **Content marketing:** This is one of the media through which we can elaborate on the concept of not-for-profit marketing. The aim of content marketing is to tell the story of the growth of the organization to the real world. When stated well through valuable content, others will want to be a part of the story in addition to your existing supporters.

- The content quality and presentation is important. The content should be concise, well-edited, and formatted. Also, try to split it up with viewable images. The images that highlight the organization's activities are effective eye-catching moments for the audiences. Also, do not forget to optimize your content for mobiles.

- The more content you put on, the more you will see that an organization has something to say. This means creating informative articles, fact sheets, and other digital resources on a regular basis will make your organization a great source of inspiration in the mind of audiences. This approach will result in a better cause and will deliver results in a fruitful manner in the form of getting the connection of more and more audiences or users.

- **Regular engagement with supporters:** It is one of the best practices to say *thank you* to your supporters. To receive follow up donations from supporters is are encouraging and appreciative moments. Once you send a thank you to your supporters over the social media platforms, they become happier and further acknowledge you and your organization with valuable greetings. The best practice is that you can even create automated e-mail responses that reduce the amount of work required on your part and also cover the objective of sending an acknowledgment to your supporters without any miss.

- **Website:** The best approach to make any organization presentable is through websites. Your website should be clear and easy to navigate as should be your e-mail and other marketing materials. To maximize lead generation and gift revenue, websites play a very important role in marketing. For example, adding pop-ups to your site is a good way to get people to sign up for your newsletters and to collect the contact information of potential users or audiences. By following this approach in your websites, your organization will improve its chances of securing new and recurring gifts from supporters and potential audiences. Those same supporters will be more interested in hearing about your recent activities and successes, and when you acknowledge their support, they'll be more likely to share your content via their social media channels and to remember you the next time you ask them to make a gift or donation.

Conclusion

In this chapter, we have discussed the history of marketing and its evolution from one version to another. We also walked through the importance, scope, and elements of marketing. We discussed the comparisons between marketing and sales. In addition to that, we highlighted the benefits and opportunities of digital marketing and its use in business-to-business (B2B), business-to-consumer (B2C), and not-for-profit (NFP) marketing. In the next chapter, we will see the working of search marketing and the importance of search engine optimization for business websites.

Points to remember

- Digital marketing is a broader term that utilizes the internet and other digital technologies to reach consumers. The basic objective is to give promotion to products and services through various forms of digital media.

- Traditional marketing performs its activities through offline mode. It has limited ability to reach customers.

- Content marketing refers to the target online audience. It is a kind of marketing that focuses on making, printing, and sharing content for online users.

- Leads generation is one of the methods which falls under the category of advertising. In marketing terminology, it is the initiative of user inquiry or interest related to the product or services offered by an organization or company.

MCQs

1. **Delivering different messages to members of a business decision-making unit is a key difference between B2C and B2B marketing which is reflected in web design through** _____.

    a) Different feature stories appealing to different members of the audience

    b) Content referencing the needs of companies of different sizes

    c) Different navigation options appealing to different members of the audience

    d) Questions on a form enquiring about the status of the business in the purchase decision process

2. **A longer decision-making process that for many consumer products is a key difference between B2C and B2B marketing which is reflected in web design through** _____.

    a) Content referencing the needs of companies of different sizes

    b) Questions on a form enquiring about the status of the business in the purchase decision process

    c) Different feature stories appealing to different members of the audience

    d) Different navigation options appealing to different members of the audience

3. **The** _____ **goal of a business-to-business website involves an interactive dialogue with a virtual salesperson.**

    a) Selling

    b) Sizzling

    c) Speaking

    d) Saving

4. The _____ goal of a business-to-business website involves gaining permission from a website visitor to engage in future dialogue by e-mail and other communications channels.

   a) Serving
   b) Speaking
   c) Selling
   d) Saving

5. Business-to business (B2B) e-commerce involves commercial transactions between an organization and other organizations (inter-organizational marketing).

   a) True
   b) False

Answers

1. *c*
2. *b*
3. *a*
4. *b*
5. *a*

Questions

1. What is digital marketing? Explain.
2. How can you categorize digital marketing?
3. Do you think digital marketing will completely replace traditional marketing in the near future?
4. How do you stay updated with the latest digital marketing trends?
5. Why is online marketing preferred over offline marketing?

Key terms

Digital marketing: It refers to the method of promoting products, services, or brands using electronic media. It normally takes place on the online platform, that is, the internet.

CHAPTER 2
Search Engine Optimization – The Core of Digital Marketing

SEO stands for search engine optimization. It is the process or technique of gaining traffic, visibility, and rank on search engines through both paid and unpaid efforts. SEO is a set of rules for optimizing your website for search engines and improve your search engine rankings. So how does search marketing function in the digital era? What is the current scenario of search engine optimization? You will find the answer to these questions in chapter this and the subsequent ones. So let's get started!

Structure

In this chapter, we will cover the following topics:

2.1   Introduction to search engine

2.2   Search engine optimization

2.3   Importance of SEO for business websites

2.4   Search results and positioning

2.5   Benefits of search positioning

2.6   Role of keywords in SEO

Objective

By thoroughly studying this chapter, you will be able to:

- Understand the importance of search engine optimization
- Understand the benefits of search positioning
- Understand the concept of various categories of linking and on-Page and off-page optimization

2.1 Introduction to search engine

Search engine can be referred to as a huge database of resources that are available on the internet such as web pages, newsgroups, images, videos, programs, and so on. It helps to find information on the World Wide Web. Users can reach out to any information by passing queries in the form of keywords or phrases.

2.2. Search Engine Optimization

SEO stands for "Search Engine Optimization." Basically, it is a technique by the implementation of which we can drive traffic directly from the search engine in a *"free," "organic," "editorial,"* or *"natural"* manner in the form of search results on search engines.

SEO or search engine optimization is a set of rules for optimizing your website or a web page for search engines so that you can improve your search engine rankings. It is the best way to increase the quality and reliability of your website by making it more user-friendly, easier to navigate, and faster than before.

SEO can be considered as a complete framework since the whole process has a set of rules (or guidelines), a number of stages, and a set of controls over your website(s). *Figure 2.1* highlights the various roles of SEO in marketing strategies such as keywords research, links building, sitemap optimization, web design, social network, content development, ranking, website optimization, etc.

Figure 2.1: *Role of search engine optimization*

All major search engines such as Google, Yahoo, Ask, etc. have a primary search results section or we can say more precisely a primary search result page, where websites, web pages, and other content such as local listings, videos, or images are shown and ranked based on what the search engine prefers to show to the users based on their previous searches and feedback. Payment isn't involved as it is with search engine marketing which we will discuss in the upcoming sections.

2.3 Importance of SEO for business websites

If you have an online store or if you provide any kind of services over the internet, then SEO can help you grow your website as well as your business and will generate enormous leads. Search engine optimization is very important because users do trust the search engines and if a website or a web page has a presence in the top position for the keywords that the user is searching or is interested in, it can archive the trust of the user more quickly.

Search engine optimization is important because of the following reasons:

- The major part of search engine traffic/users are more likely to click on one of the top five results in the results pages: **search engine result page (SERP).** To get the advantage of this and gain more traffic or visitors to your website or customers to your online store, your website needs to appear in that top portion of the search result page of the search engine.

- SEO is not only for optimizing your website for search engines. Besides that, good SEO practices can improve the user experience and usability of a website.

- Users do depend on search engines and if your website shows up in the top positions for the keywords or phrases that the user tries to find, it increases the website's trust also.

- SEO can improve your website's promotions on social media. People who find your website by searching on search engines like Google or Yahoo are more likely to promote it on Facebook, Twitter, or other social media channels.

- SEO is significant for the smooth running of a website that has a huge amount of data. If you have two or more admin or authors, then SEO can benefit you in a direct and indirect way. The direct benefit is increased search engine traffic the and indirect benefit is having a common agenda/checklists to use whenever you are about to publish content on the website.

- SEO can give you an extra edge in the competition. If two websites or your rival's website is providing the same services or selling the same thing that you are, the SEO friendly website will definitely have more visitors/customers and make more sales.

2.4 Search results and positioning

To make your website active and operational, it is necessary that some positive and preventive steps should be taken in the direction of placing and looking at the outcomes.

- If you manage to get a good position in the search engine results page, then it will result in tremendously increased overall targeted visitors/traffic and is a result of a proper SEO strategy.

- More commonly, this happens just due to having a search engine optimization specialist or SEO service working behind the website.

- Better search engine positioning can be the result of a thorough search engine optimization strategy, all with the view of maximizing your website's visibility search.

- Implementation of the proper positioning strategy can result in achieving the websites' core online business goals, namely improved new customer/client achieving rates.

- This can be achieved by implementing thorough website search engine optimization rules/guidelines to solely manage all parts of your website relating to search engine algorithms, and how those algorithms will react to the content of your website.

- This crucial step ensures that the engines will position your site properly within relevant search results.

- Every website has different challenges to face in order to obtain great positioning within search results. These challenges might be related to the design of the website or to the core business agenda of your online store or the service that you provide.

- Just like the firm's business agenda, the marketing plan must have a positioning strategy planned to match the corporate goals for the website.

- This strategy must also include the optimization of the text areas (meta tags, title tags, description, etc of the website as well as any needful source code adjustments to make the website "search friendly" for the search engines.

- Making changes in the HTML code of your website should not normally affect the end users' experience of how they use it or see it. These changes may include a correction in the scripts, adding navigation elements, or making minor textual adjustments as needed to ensure that you are found under a more relevant keyword or phrase.

- In the beginning, when you apply your SEO technique, you have to dedicate many hours studying each of your competitor's websites so your online business can reach its maximum potential in the search results.

- If you have managed to attain a rank at the top position in the engine results, it does not mean that the work is over.

- Your rivals will be watching, and they will definitely want to return themselves to the position in the search results that is giving you a tremendous amount of traffic to your website. Therefore, you must do the optimization in a consistent manner. Therefore, ongoing optimization is essential.

- Search engines frequently do changes in their indices, drop and add websites, and update the search algorithms in order to improve the overall relevance of their results.

- To ensure a continued strong and improved positioning, a maintenance program is required in the period of a month.

- Your SEO strategy must include a procedure that will help your site to stay on top of the constantly updating/changing algorithms and that works to maintain or improve your placement.

- Make sure your business doesn't fall due to these kind of low poles. Ensure that it has a proper ongoing optimization strategy from time to time.

2.5 Benefits of search positioning

There are various benefits of search positioning such as:

1) **User-friendly websites**

   SEO will help you to get the owner of the business to create a faster, smoother, and user-friendlier website. Although majority of the people still hang around the old definition of SEO and think that it is only for optimizing your website for the search engines, SEO is today also about improving user experiences.

   Clean, well-structured, and uncluttered websites compel a casual visitor to spend more time on the website, decreasing bounce rate and increasing page views. Similarly, more relevant content (blog articles and sales pages) keeps your visitors/readers happy and engages them as they are more likely to find answers to their questions, solve their issues, and helps them find exactly what they are looking for on your website.

If on-page SEO is done properly, it can make your users happy which leads to search engines picking your website more frequently in that keyword/phrase search result page as they (search engines) love to serve high-quality information to their users.

2) It brings in more customers

One of the major reasons for having a website is to stand out from your rival's website and increase your customer base. Otherwise, it makes no sense to invest thousands of rupees on marketing. The business websites that are well-SEO optimized websites bring in more and more customers and grow faster than businesses that do not have one.

SEO is the most affordable and efficient marketing strategy that can be used today. Moreover, it will only bring in customers who are really finding your product or service.

If you're willing to give few hours of your time, a small amount of money, and some energy, SEO will help you bring in more targeted customer/traffic to your website as well as more customers to your business than any other marketing strategy you'll ever use.

3) Better conversion rates

Websites that are SEO optimized load faster and display properly in almost all types of devices and display sizes including tablets, PCs, laptops, mobiles, and are easy to read and surf. Websites that are easy to read and navigate have more chances of having and holding the attention of your readers/visitors, that is, there are more chances that they will become your loyal visitors, subscribers, and returning customers.

4) Builds your brand awareness

One of the key advantages of getting higher rankings on the **SERP** is building brand awareness. When your sites appear on the first page of major search engines such as Google,

Bing, and Yahoo, your potential visitors/customers are more likely to trust your brand when they search for a particular keyword or phrase rather than your competitors that don't have a strong presence on the web.

That is why business owners who want to build great brand awareness (either globally or expanding locally) must invest in SEO and start gaining top rankings for the keyword/phrases related to their business. Things have changed a lot; search engines now play a major role in breaking or making your brand.

5) **Bypass your competition.**

Suppose that two businesses that are in the same industry are selling similar products and are listed at similar prices. One of them has done SEO properly on the website while the other does not have an SEO website. Let us say everything else is equal. Which company do you think will get more visitors/customers on their website from searches? Which company will grow faster and become more successful? The answer to the respective questions is the one that has SEO. Search engines and SEO are very powerful. If other businesses are doing SEO, you must simply ask yourself why you haven't invested in such a strategy yet as well.

2.6 Role of keywords in SEO

The importance of keywords in SEO is in part due to their importance outside of it. Forget about rankings, traffic, keywords, or even your website. If you really knew your true customers' feelings, how would you operate your business correctly? How valuable would those insights be to your business website? What about the time that we are searching?

The answer to these key questions is as follows:

The combination of anonymousness and immediate access to a wealth of information paves the way for an unadulterated look into what we truly want.

It's a data-driven truth serum.

As we know, keyword research is the most powerful research tool that can be beneficial in many different ways, not just for informing about website content. To get the most out of keywords, you have to look beyond the literal translation and also explicitly pick up on the implicit clues to grow the true intent of each keyword.

Keywords are like personas.

A persona acts as a bulls-eye. They aren't all that we are after but by aiming for them, we're ensuring ourselves for success.

2.7 Meta tags and meta description

Meta description tag: *"The tag in HTML that is used to summarize a web page's content in the 160 character snippet"*. Search engines sometimes use these meta description tags in the search results page to let visitors know what a page is about before clicking on it. In this example, we will look at how search engines use meta descriptions, what the top SEO blogs say about meta descriptions, whether they really use the meta description tags, and the reasons why we should use them.

Let's take examples of meta descriptions and how search engines use them. We'll look at Google's own Meta description:

```
<meta name="description" content="Search the world's
information, including web pages, images, videos and
more. Google has many special features to help you
find exactly what you're looking for.">
```

It is exactly 159 characters, including spaces. Google's meta description is displayed like this in the top three search engines.

Most SEO's might ask, *"What if meta descriptions do not count into the rankings algorithm? Why should I use them then?"* The answer is, *"Instead of thinking about them as a ranking factor on the search engine, start thinking about them as a conversion factor for your business."*

Here are some more good reasons to still keep your meta description as a priority on your website including your internal pages, homepage, blog posts, and so on.

Reason 1: Bolded keywords in search results.

Reason 2: Top social networks use them.

Reason 3: Social bookmarking networks use them.

2.8 On-page and off-page optimization

Improvement in the websites is one of the fundamental needs of functionality in the digital world. There are two major approaches that are preferred in the optimization process, namely on-page and off-page. *Figure 2.2* discusses the scenario of both techniques which are suitable for the entities as per their desire and demand.

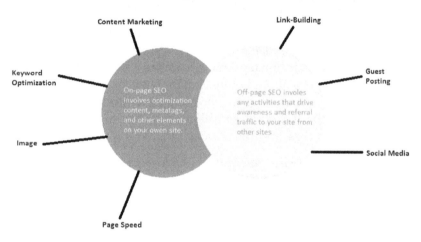

Figure 2.2: On-page and off-page SEO Scenario

The aim of both on-page and off-page methodologies is to connect the users to their respective domains in an efficient and timely manner. A brief description with exemplary content is as follows:

2.8.1 On-page SEO (also known as "on-site" SEO)

It is the technique of optimizing different parts of your website that are important for your rankings in search engines. It's your stuff that you can change and have control over your own website.

Here are some main factors that are included:

- **Title tags**

  Tags are one of the vital factors that help in website management through the on-page SEO methodology. Your target keywords should be placed in the title tag of each and every page of the corresponding website.

- **Headings**

  The largest word size is usually represented through headings. The main aim of a heading is to highlight the theme of the main content. Even the search engines give high priority to headings in comparison to other page contents. On-page SEO suggests working more on headings while keeping the fact in mind that the overall content of the web pages will be conducted rightly.

- **URL framework**

  On-page SEO experts always suggest working on the stability factor of the URL framework. Professionals suggest keeping your URLs unaltered as much as you can. To avail the benefit of the URL framework, always try to place target keywords into the URL platform. If possible, try to avoid changing URLs in a frequent manner unless it is necessary. As an exceptional case, if a change of URL is required, then work on redirecting the old URL to the new URL.

- **Description**

  On-page SEO suggests using "alt text" for images. To add description related to the images that exist as part of website content, it is best practice to apply the respective label naming. Most relevant keywords and descriptions related to images help search engines in understanding the theme and content of your web pages more actively and easily.

- **Keyword density**

  The right selection and density of the keyword is another challenge for site development. This restriction is overcomed by the strategic approach of on-page optimization. The best way is the right selection and length of keywords. The appropriate word which properly covers the meaning of the entire content of the page should be preferred. Moreover, the length of the keyword should be as minimal as it can be.

- **Keyword Placement**

  The usage of keyword and its placement is another important factor that was taken care of by on-page SEO in a very efficient manner. The placement of keyword in the right position and link is the valid approach taken care of by SEO expertise on the basis of background details and other relevant information of the respective websites.

- **Page load speed**

  The speed of page loading should be appropriate. To provide memorable user experience and also to access the website repetitively by the user, it is necessary that we optimize the website and its related web pages regularly. This practice will help in gaining higher rank during the phase of the search engine result page.

- **Page content**

  The content of the page is the key element. The success and popularity of the website are directly proportional to the quality of the content of the web page. If the user searches for some specific information on your web page, then they must be able to get that information in a very fruitful and knowledgeable manner. The content of the page should be clear, readable, and easily understandable.

- **Internal linking**

  Internal linking is the backbone of a website. For smooth navigation or movement from one web page to the other web pages of the website, internal linking plays an important role. It helps visitors in fetching relevant information from alternative pages of the website. Moreover, it also helps in increasing the number of visitors not only on the home page but also on other respective pages of the website.

  By operating or engaging in on-page SEO, search engines can easily identify the source or origin of your website, the index of web pages, the layout of the website, and further rank your website based on the search engine result page.

Figure 2.3 highlights the various components associated with on-page SEO and off-page SEO.

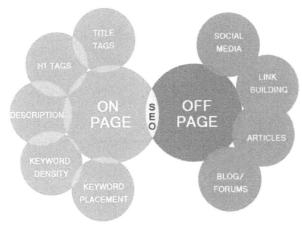

Figure 2.3: *Categories of on-page and off-page SEO*

2.8.2 Off-Page SEO

Off-page SEO is everything that does not happen directly to your website. It includes activities like social media, link building, blogs or forums, and so on.

One of the best SEO strategies is to create backlinks. They help in raising the domain as well as the page authority of your website. Consider the example of a bathtub filled with water. In this case, we put some rubber ducks in a bathtub and start filling the bathtub with water. Here, consider the ducks as your web pages and the water as backlinks. With this presumption, we move ahead with the proceedings. Now when you start filling the bathtub with water, your rubber ducks will rise to the level at the top of the bathtub. In short, initially, the rubber ducks are placed at the bottom level or base level of the bathtub, but once the level of water rises, the rubber ducks' level is also raised from bottom to high. The same approach is observed during the procedure of off-site optimization. The website's popularity and increase in its page rank activity are based on the above-highlighted example. The domain authority parameter takes care of how authoritative your websites are in comparison to other websites out there.

Figure 2.4 demonstrates the concept of page rank: *"The more links your website has, the higher your pages rank."*

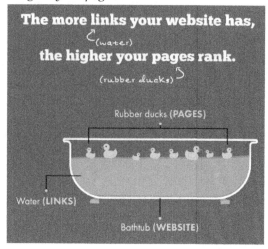

Figure 2.4: *Concept of page rank*

The major factors for off-page SEO are the quality of the backlinks and how many backlinks you have to your website/web page. Some of the ways by which you can build links to your website/web pages are as follows:

- Creating great content so that everyone really wants to link to it because it is valuable.

- In today's world, social media can play a major role by getting shares of your content that ultimately generates links.

- Reach out to the top influencers in your industry by e-mail, digital marketing strategies, etc. That will ultimately link to you.

- Guest blogging on sites that are related to your website or in the same domain/industry as you. Through this, the guest posts will have some more backlinks to your website.

While the quantity of links is still an important factor, SEO professionals and content creators are realizing that the quality of links is now more important than the quantity of links you that have. However, creating shareable content is still the very first step in order to get valuable links and improving your off-page SEO.

Now the key question arises: How many links do you really need for good off-page SEO?

That is a tough question to answer and somewhat depends upon the domain authority of your competitor's website since you really want to make sure you're playing in the same industry.

Some business owners take the help of SEO in buying backlinks so that their domain becomes popular in much less time and further attracts users to access their domain through their dramatically raised page ranking scenario. However, most of the search engines will penalize for an illegal attempt at manipulating the page rankings. As per the ethics of link building, quality is more important than quantity. Keeping this principle in mind, if you submit your links to other types of link directories whose sole purpose is to raise your domain authority, then in that case, a strict action will be taken against this violation.

2.9 Backlink

When one web page/website gets a link from another web page/website, then that link is called as a **backlink**. A backlink makes a massive impact on a website's position in search engine result pages. This is why backlinks are considered a very crucial factor in improving a website's SEO and search engine ranking. Search engines consider multiple perimeters to decide the search engine ranking of any web page or website on SERP. No one knows exactly how much weight do search engines really give to backlinks when listing results. However, we do know that they are very important for certain things.

Backlinks should be authentic. This means that a website must not use any kind of unethical or artificial ways to create backlinks for their website(s). The quality of links is way more important than the quantity of them.

For example: Website ABC is a restaurant's website and it takes a backlink from website XYZ which is a well-known food review blog or website. This is an ethical, valuable, and relevant backlink that website ABC has gained.

Since backlinks are important, there are lots of unethical practices followed by website owners to get backlinks. Some of these practices include selling backlinks, link exchange networks, purchasing backlinks, and so on. Most of these ways of backlinking are not recommended by search engines. They mostly penalize and deindex websites suspected of involvement in such kinds of unethical practices. Backlinks are like conversations among websites.

2.10 Internal and external links

Internal links, also known as inbound links, are hyperlinks that direct or we can say redirect the visitor/reader to a specific (target) page of your website; whereas an external link is a hyperlink that directs the visitor/reader to a specific page on another website. External links can seem counterintuitive. However, you don't want your valuable readers/visitors clicking on links that direct them away from your website. Linking to a high authority website/web page will also help you to appear to be an authority and can help search engines figure out what your content is really about for SEO purposes.

It's important for you to remember that other websites for different companies can also provide external links to your website in their own content. We have seen in many cases that if a company found that your blog post has useful content, then they may link back to it as a source for their own blog. These types of links to your site can be a jackpot for your website/blog post as they boost your ranking in search engines using a search algorithm.

Benefits of internal links

More and more internal links on a web page will help a reader/ visitor to stay more and engage with your website longer. This may lead them to become a permanent reader/customer/follower of your website. These links are more accessible to the readers/visitors and they increase the page authority of the web pages and the overall website. Internal links are usually used as a call-to-action. For example, the reader/visitor might be prompted to learn or read more about a topic by following that internal link or else a reader may be asked to contact you or schedule a meeting.

Adding internal links in your website/web page will also improve visibility and rank on a search engine. For the text of the hyperlink, the anchor text should be more to the point and an in-depth group of words that will help a search engine bot to "crawl" or understand your web page more effectively. Internal linking will help a bot of the search engine to find other web pages on your website too. It is seen that a web page that is easy to navigate for a reader/visitor and search engine bots is properly indexed.

This means that the web page will also be added to the search engine's search result pages so that your site can be easily found by the end-users as shown in *Figure 2.5* which indicates the concept of internal link.

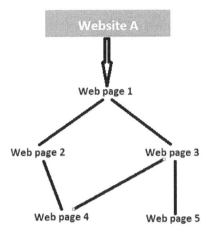

Figure 2.5: Concept of internal link

Benefits of external links

The number of external backlinks and quality of those external links that you use is shown on your web page or website matter. Adding informative and trustworthy links of websites that are of high quality to your web pages will help you improve the credibility of your website, whereas adding poor-quality links might make a bad impact on your site. Linking to other web pages/websites will not make any bad impact on your page rank as long as the relatable content you're backlinking to comes from high authority websites. An external link has more value if it is linked to relevant and popular web pages that are related to the content that your web page has and is highly ranked in the search engine.

Valuable external links can be proved as a key factor in improving the authority of your website by providing a reader with references as shown in *Figure 2.6*.

Figure 2.6: Concept of external link

Whenever you link to another web page/website, that web page/ website can see that you're linking to them. Then, there are some chances when they return the favour by linking to your site in their content as well. External links are also sometimes considered as outbound links from other websites that link to your web page/ website, further improving your website's reliability as well as the credibility because they prove that the content of your website is valuable. External links are a great way to make connections, reach out, and get your content out there where it deserves to be. This type of external link is a good source of ethical or free traffic for your web page/website, and as mentioned above, is a crucial element of search engine algorithms such as Google's search algorithm and Yahoo's as well.

2.11 Ranking

In SEO, *"Rankings refers to the position of a website in the search engine results page."* There are various ranking factors that make an impact on search engines such as whether a website should appear higher on the SERP based on the content relevancy to the searched keyword or phrase or the quality of backlinks that a page has. The following factors might be closely connected to the ranking factor:

- Sitemap and internal linking.
- Page loading time (site speed).
- The way of using keywords/phrases in text elements like meta descriptions, meta titles, text elements (main content), and so on.
- Optimization of the terms of the content based on comparison with other documents on the same topic (proof and relevant terms, topic/content clusters, WDF*IDF).
- URL structure.
- Trust assigned to the page.
- Number of backlinks.
- CTR in the SERPs, that is, how often users click on the result and consider other factors like page traffic, authorship, how up-to-date a page is, and so on.
- Bounce rate and time on site.

2.12 SEO sitemap

In general terms, *"An XML sitemap is a list of total URLs of the website."* It is like a roadmap for the search engines to give them information about what content is available and how to reach it.

In *Figure 2.7*, a search engine will find all the nine pages that are in your sitemap with the help of the XML sitemap file as shown below. On the website, the search engine will have to jump through five internal links to get to that page. XML site maps are a vital element of websites as they help in framing the architecture and are further capable of updating the content of present as well as new pages.

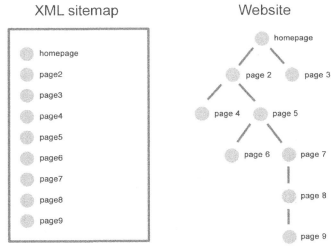

Figure 2.7: Layout of SEO site map

The XML site map is especially important for websites that:

- Have deep website architecture and/or thousands of pages.
- Lack a strong external link profile.
- Frequently update the content of existing pages.
- Suffer from weak internal linking and orphan pages.
- Frequently add new pages.

Note: Submitting a site map with no-index URLs can also speed up the de-indexation process of that URL. This can be more efficient than removing URLs in the Google Search console if you have many to be de-indexed. But use this with care and make sure that you only add such URLs temporarily to your site maps.

2.13 Steps for B2B SEO and B2C SEO

Business to business (B2B) and **business to consumer (B2C)** markets are treated separately in many ways, including the ways in which they are marketed. In fact, because they are two different types of businesses, they will not have the same approaches. Each market includes different type of target audiences and this needs to be seen clearly in all business decisions taken. As we know, internet marketing and search engine optimization are becoming very important in both sectors. Therefore, it is necessary to understand that the strategies for each should differ as well.

Marketing campaign goals

The goals of the campaign are the main difference between a B2B and B2C SEO campaign. The process of decision-making in the B2B market generally takes longer than that of the B2C market. It is basically due to the much higher cost of a product or length of commitment to service.

Therefore, a B2B SEO campaign needs to grow awareness about the business and generate leads that will turn into sales in the long run. Sometimes, the goal is to get the visitor to sign up for a newsletter, download the information, or fill out the lead form for the sales team that they can use to follow up.

On the other side, the goal of most B2C websites, specifically those with an e-commerce component, is to change those visitors into paying customers by immediate purchase from the website. These differing goals make a huge difference in all the decisions made throughout the SEO process.

Keyword selection process

One of the most major parts of an SEO campaign structure is the keyword selection process. Since in the B2B sector, the buying decision takes longer and is more complex, a B2B company needs to involve keywords/phrases that attract the audience and make them take action at different parts of the cycle.

This means that keyword (or phrase) research is vaster and should integrate keywords for both transactional and informational search. Since B2B keyword research mostly targets a smaller, niche audience, the terminology can usually be more technical. The B2C keyword (or phrase) research process can also be said to be complex because the search volume is very high. A B2C company needs to figure out the right keywords or phrases that aren't too niche or too broad and find that sweet spot that will convert the quality visitors into leads and that will result in conversions.

Figure 2.8 communicates the SEO process of link building in both domains, that is, B2B and B2C companies:

Figure 2.8: *Layout of link building*

After the completion of keyword research and when selected keywords have been integrated and implemented on all pages of the website, the next step will be link building in the SEO process for B2B and B2C companies. B2C links usually grow at a faster speed since there is a huge audience base. B2B companies need to work more for their links. In order to attract the attention of the search engine bots, link building is all about grabbing the attention of your target traffic. The online behavior of a B2B audience and a B2C audience are different in many aspects.

It is important to do proper research to figure out where they can perform amazingly and frequently pursue getting links in those places. A B2C audience usually spends most of their time using social media to find products that they want while on the other hand, a B2B audience spends most of their time browsing and reading blogs to find more information. A diverse link building technique raises the chances of being seen.

Here's a list of the elements of SEO marketing of B2B and B2C that are the same:

1) **On-site optimization**

   No matter what type of business you have, the process of implementation of on-site optimization remains the same but with some differences. While the strategy used in keyword research can be different between these two (B2B and B2C companies), the rest of the elements that need to be optimized are still the same.

   These elements include:

   - **Heading tag:** The <h1> tag should be similar to or same as the page's title tag.

   - **Title tags:** Every page on the website should have a unique title tag for it.

   - **Description tag:** Even though this isn't a ranking factor, it's still a major element that helps in generating more click-through.

   - **Body content:** Whether you have a B2C or B2B website, the body content must be optimized regularly.

2) **Content**

   The process of writing great content is a core part of a great SEO program. It doesn't matter whether you have a B2C company or a B2B company, great writing must be taken seriously. You will have to create content that targets potential costumers/visitors in each part of the sales cycle and also write pieces that current customers will find a use for. By doing this, you'll not only be creating content that will bring traffic/customers to your website directly from the search engines, but it will also grow your reach and engagement on different social media platforms.

   There are a few elements of every SEO program that stay the same whether you have a B2B or a B2C company. However, there are some differences between some specific parts of the SEO process between these two, including the way you build links and research keywords.

2.14 Advantages and disadvantages of SEO

Search engine optimization (SEO) is a strategy of optimization which is very free and effective as well. SEO is useful for the smooth functioning of your web page/website. SEO is used to grow and measure the number of users/visitors to a web page/website by getting a high-ranking in the search engine's **search results page (SERP)** like Google, Yahoo, Bing, and other web search engines. Search engine optimization revolves around content writing, keywords research, web pages, positioning of the keyword(s), ranking, and optimized links.

The advantages of search engine optimization are as follows:

- **It is free of cost.** SEO does not believe in paid advertisement techniques, but all of the methods need time. It is seen that for many businesses, it is not possible to give more time to SEO due to different scenarios but the web page/website ranked on your main or targeted keywords can make good money.

- **Builds high brand integrity.** Studies have shown that frequent advertisements can be annoying and lots of users use ad blockers integrated into their apps these days. SEO is one of the great methods when it comes to creating a brand identity on the internet. Longer articles that have approximately 1,200 to 1,500 words in their content perform far better in search engines generally. Laetsch states, "It is now different than it had been 2 or 3 decades ago when 300 phrases long blog was considered a reasonably long page. Long length articles get more visitors, and they rank comparatively higher than the small length articles in SEO. The modifications that search engines like Google, Yahoo, Bing, and so on are creating day-by-day, and why they are pushing these updates, would be to be certain they are sending traffic/visitors to web pages which humans like to read."

Figure 2.9 demonstrates the effects of SEO on websites such as increased traffic, more leads/sales, exposure, brand credibility, and improved rankings.

Figure 2.9: *SEO effects*

- **People do rely on search results.** If you manage to appear high in the search result page of the search engine, then it may result in growth in conversion rates and greater ROI.

- **Those who search (users) are often ready to buy.** Searchers are generally those people who search for terms like *"mobile phone repair service in India,"* and they are most likely to speak to somebody and make a decision. This usually means you will be using your time earning more targeted and prospective customers.

- **Results are long-lasting.** Online searchers generally see more of those sites which are in the maximum priority in the result page with this rundown since they visit those that are relevant to their search query. Have you ever asked why some of the websites rank higher no matter what they post? You need to understand that it is due to SEO. Web optimization is a way by which search engines detect and rank your own page higher compared to the different web pages in that research query.

Research by *Oxford Economics for Virgin Media Business* asserts that the UK economy may attain a growth of 92 billion if companies completely develop their digital capacities. It states that the UK business will add millions of new jobs in the upcoming years by enhancing their electronic abilities.

- **You can get targeted traffic.** It may be said that you really don't pay for the action and motion era, especially in the same way that people do when using paid advertising methods such as the **pay-per-click (PPC)** method of Google AdWords. Your price will entirely decrease on the off probability that you perform all other search engine optimization practices like third-party referencing and age. By the use of analytics and reporting programs, you will clearly notice a boost in traffic/visitors. This is a clear way by which you can make most of the efforts for your company. SEO will give you great results. You will begin your search engine optimization efforts effectively and the traffic/visitors will also increase at a steady speed. There are so many tools available in the market to monitor and observe the traffic/visitors to your website and you can straight-away observe as more visitors/people go to your website and the sales goes through the same roof.

- **SEO encourages business growth.** It is estimated that there were approximately 2.2 trillion searches created in the Google search engine in the year 2018. That's approximately *5,922,000,000* searches created per day.

  SEO can boost the growth of your company and provide you better ROI than ordinary advertisements.

The disadvantages of search engine optimization are as follows:

- **It requires some time.** Updating might take search engines like Google, Yahoo, and so on time. Searching for dependable articles and using one blog article won't be enough to put your website into the very best of outcomes. It takes some time to see development and so, the return on investment (ROI). SEO requires investment and patience. On the other side, in addition, it tells you that if you stop taking actions, it will take some more time for one to drop in search results too.

- **Take note.** If a company claims that it can provide fast results, don't believe it. They might use "unethical" methods that may harm your website (domain authority and page authority) in the very long run.

- **There's no guarantee.** You can come across many non-relevant variables around search results and competition keywords, and we can never completely understand how each search engine algorithm works. Therefore, there are no guaranteed effects. To boost your business, you have to be ready to focus on the more niche markets and product areas.

- **You may be penalized.** If you submit your links to any other of link directories whose sole purpose is to raise your domain authority, then in that case, a strict action will be taken against this violation.

Conclusion

In this chapter, we have discussed the concept of search engine optimization. We also went through the importance, scope, and elements of marketing. We discussed the concept of page ranking. In addition, we presented the categories of on-page and off-page search engine optimization.

In the next chapter, we will go through an overview of e-mail marketing and the importance of digital display advertising.

Points to remember

- Improved search engine positioning is the result of a thorough search engine marketing and website optimization strategy, all with an eye for maximizing your search visibility.

- SEO is an opening for getting movement from the free search results on a web search tool.

- It is helpful for the smooth running of your site. SEO is utilized to expand the measure of visitors to a website by getting a high-ranking arrangement in the search results page of a search engine which includes Google, Bing, Yahoo, and other web search engines.

- Search engine optimization is about keywords, positioning, optimizing links, content, pages, and rank. Content marketing is a form of marketing focused on creating, publishing, and distributing content for a targeted audience online.

MCQs

1. **Which on-page element carries the most weight for SEO?**

   a) The meta keywords tag

   b) The title tag

   c) The headers (H1, H2, H3, etc.)

   d) None of the above

2. **What do the acronyms PA, DA, and PR stand for?**

   a) Personal authority, domain authority, parked rename

   b) Page authority, domain age, page rank

   c) Page authority, domain authority, page rank

   d) None of the above

3. **Which of the following tactics can harm your search rankings?**

   a) Adding navigation links to your page's template

   b) Using text that is the same color as your page's background

   c) Linking to your site from other websites

   d) None of the above

4. **The number of characters recommended for title tag?**

   a) 120

   b) 250

   c) 70

   d) 100

5. **How much time period is required to get a Google page ranking?**

   a) 2 weeks

   b) 1 week

   c) 2 months

   d) More than 3 months

Answers

1. *b*
2. *c*
3. *b*
4. *c*
5. *d*

Questions

1. How do you measure SEO success?
2. How do you approach keyword research?
3. What is link building and why does it matter?
4. What is on-page versus off-page SEO?
5. What is the relationship between SEO and SEM?

Key terms

Search Engine Optimization: It is an approach that is used as one of the digital marketing strategies in enhancing page ranking and also to raise the purity and trustworthiness of the website by applying its effect in site mapping and link building.

CHAPTER 3
E-mail Marketing and Digital Display Advertising

E-mail marketing is a precious and reasonable way for business owners to promote their brand, products, and services. It allows them to approach customers and build a solid relationship with them. What is the structure and delivery mechanism of e-mail? How is the e-mail campaign created and measured? What is the concept of A/B testing and its use in e-mail marketing? You will find the answer to these questions in this chapter and the subsequent ones. So let's get started!

Structure

In this chapter, we will cover the following topics:

Objective

After studying this chapter, you should be able to:

- Understand the importance of e-mail marketing
- Learn to create an e-mail campaign and its measurement
- Understand the concepts, benefits, and challenges of digital display advertising

3.1 Introduction to e-mail marketing

E-mail marketing is a manner through which you can connect to users in order to retain their interest in your products. If your call to action is active and your follow up is consistent, you can proceed in the right direction of a positive campaign. It is one of the vital sections of any organization in its corresponding digital marketing strategies.

It involves using e-mail to give promotion to products and services with the purpose of enhancing a relationship with the present as well as new customers. This strategy helps in achieving market targets.

The main objective of e-mail marketing is to strengthen customer loyalty and extend the business with faith and brand awareness.

3.2 Elements of e-mail

There are various approaches that help in understanding the overall functionality of e-mail marketing. The varying elements of e-mail are as follows:

- **Send e-mails in a professional way.**

  It is a very sensitive matter to understand the emotional side of users or potential customers. The users received multiple e-mails on a daily basis. They are regularly struggling with the inbox section in order to keep controlled. For example, if you committed to sending one e-mail per week but instead send them (users or clients) emails on a daily basis, then you are placing yourself in the direction of failure.

- **Use a customized subject line.**

  It is good practice to customize your e-mail subject line. Rather than sending an e-mail blindly to any user or client, first create a cluster of users of similar interest. Once your group is created based on similar user behavior and need, segment your e-mail list to the corresponding group.

  Being one of the elements of e-mail, the management of the subject line is very important. A customized subject line is more likely to be opened in comparison to alternative cases. The best approach is to use the recipient's first name and further address their specific needs. In addition, with the help of an e-mail service provider and marketing tool, you can insert the first name in the subject.

- **Segment your lists to send more targeted e-mails.**

  Segmentation is one of the best practices that has been followed in the surroundings of e-mail marketing. For business expansion, such type of an approach is to be proceeded with. Without the concept of segmentation, it becomes difficult to engage the targeted users. Generally, users receive multiple e-mails on a daily basis in which most of them are not relevant to them. To overcome this situation, segmentation show its true colors by increasing connection of the recipients. Segmenting the lists to your targeted users via e-mail will increase faith and interest towards the sender and the related e-mail content.

- **Include one clear call to action.**

  E-mails need to have one clear call to action. The content of an e-mail should be simple, clear, and short. Do not blast your users with exhaustive information for action. Because of that, they become confused or disconnected. Consider e-mail to be an opportunistic platform not as a one-time go activity. They have the characteristics of landing pages wherein your aim should be for the users to take a specific move relatively fast towards your message.

- **A well written e-mail copy should be short, concise, and should encourage engagement.**

  A well-written e-mail is always short, simple, and focused towards its content of description. As per the study, it came to notice that on an average, a user scans e-mails in just 51 seconds. To catch our user or audience, the well-written approach of e-mail which has been discussed should be followed.

- **Personalize e-mails based on customer data.**

  It is one of the good practices to personalize e-mails formulated on either the user's first name or full name. This approach helps a lot in raising the activity to capture and engage interested users via e-mail. According to a survey by professional health bodies, human beings like hearing their own names. This survey motivates e-mail marketers to follow this technique in e-mail activity.

- **Don't send ugly e-mails.**

  Before sending e-mails, make sure that they are well-structured and optimized for various online platforms such as desktop/laptop, mobile, and so on. If your e-mails are not optimized, then the users consider such type of e-mails in the category of ugly e-mails and delete those e-mails immediately. To avoid this, a preventive measure regarding e-mail optimization should be taken care of.

- **Don't forget the unsubscribe link.**

  Adding an unsubscribe link in your e-mail is a good sign of e-mail marketing. This approach helps the marketer in understanding whether the audience is interested or not, that is, whether or not the users are finding their e-mails relevant or useful. As per research and studies, 14 percent of users unsubscribe from e-mails because they find them irrelevant or get bored of the content mentioned in the e-mails.

Mentioning an unsubscribe link will encourage you in a manner as you will keep your e-mails personalized and will send them only to the cluster of interested users. This approach will save you time and effort.

3.3 E-mail list generation

E-mail list generator is a method that obtains addresses from individuals, shares some comments or articles to the users via e-mail, creates relevant content, segments the e-mail list, provides links, and promotes offers through social media channels. The detailed description about e-mail list generation is as follows:

1) **Create remarkable e-mail content.**

   Your e-mail content should be capable enough to attract users who further share your emails to their corresponding networks. If the content is eye catching, they will always look forward to your upcoming e-mails.

2) **Encourage subscribers to share and forward your e-mails.**

   There are various ways in e-mail marketing through which you can motivate users to get in touch with you and also with their peer group or friends. First, you may include button a button namely "e-mail to a friend" in your e-mail. Secondly, you may add a text based link namely "Subscribe." With both these ways, it becomes easier to gain access not only to the existing or current users but also to their friends and networks. In this way, you can expand your contact list.

3) **Segment your e-mail lists by buyer persona.**

   Just getting stuck to single e-mail subscription will not work. It is suggested to create varying types of e-mail subscriptions so that more content can be shared to the targeted users. Although recipients are more likely to click on those e-mails that are of their interest but there is still a high probability in the case of multiple types of e-mail subscriptions, the users will to subscribe one of them.

4) Restore a stale e-mail list with an opt-in campaign.

Reinvigorate those e-mail lists that are no longer interesting or exciting with an opt-in campaign. Create an energetic and engaging opt-in message and send it to your old list. By applying this method, some of the e-mail contacts from the stale e-mail list will become active responders and some of them may still be in the category of non-responders. Remove the non-responders from your list and focus only on the active responders because only engaged contacts can improve your deliverability and increase the odds of your e-mail list generation.

5) Add a link to your employees' signatures.

To increase the frequency of users approaching the landing page, it is a good approach to hyperlink e-mail signatures. By adding links, the active users can sign up for your mailing list and can show their interest to their network also.

6) Create a new lead generation offer.

To engage more and more users, try to place some offer on your respective web page. For example, develop a list of free e-books and placed it on your landing page with an option for the visitor saying that to download the highlighted e-books freely, they may have to provide their e-mail address. This type of offer is known as "gated offer."

7) Create a free online tool or resource.

An alternative way to engage your audience is to offer free online tools or resources in your landing page. The only way through which you can achieve your targeted users is to just convey to them to provide their e-mail addresses to access all the freely available resources.

8) Create 'bonus' content.

Sometimes, to gain the interest of the targeted users, we need to offer free content first. This type of content is known as bonus content. This approach is different from a 'gated offer'. In this, we start with a blog post first that offers beginner advice on a subject in the initial phase, and then we proceed to the advanced phase of accessibility; the users are suggested to submit their e-mail addresses in the corresponding landing page.

9) **Promote an online contest.**

An activity like an online contest can be conducted on your social media account in which the users can freely register to participate, perform, and win. The offer may encourage users to participate in exchange for their contact information and e-mail addresses.

10) **Promote one of your lead generation offers on Twitter.**

Try to use different social media channels such as Twitter to promote various online offers such as a free e-book and other resources to your targeted users or followers that requires their e-mail addresses to regain them.

11) **Promote an offer through Facebook that requires an e-mail address**

Similar free online offers can be shared through the Facebook platform. Facebook has a timeline section where you can promote your information with relevant content descriptions. In addition to that, you can share some social buttons on the landing page where your followers can gain access to avail those offers for themselves as well as for their friends or networks.

12) **Add a call to action (CTA) button to the top of your Facebook business page.**

It is always recommended to add a CTA button to your respective business page. The presence of the CTA button helps you to gain access to the e-mail addresses of your potential users.

3.4 E-mail structure

The e-mail structure describes the overall framework and its functionality. Each and every component of the e-mail structure highlights some information either in limited or in the detailed description.

The structure of an e-mail consists of headers and bodies. An e-mail has some basic parts such as the message itself which consists of elements like the header fields, a set of lines describing the message's settings such as the sender, the recipient, the date and time information, recipient e-mail address, and so on.

There is a standard structure for e-mails. E-mail contents are primarily classified into two sub-parts, namely the header and the body. The details are as follows:

- **The header**

  The e-mail header is one of the important sub-parts of the e-mail structure. It provides us the unique identity of the message. In addition to that, it highlights the general details related to the message. It consists of various parts such as the subject, sender, date and time received, reply-to, forward, recipient, attachment, and so on. A brief discussion is as follows:

  o **Subject**

  This part of the header highlights the title or topic of the message. Generally, the subject part is also visible with the user's name. The subject fields are examined by the spam scanners in order to evaluate the messages.

  o **Sender (From:)**

  This header part is considered to be the source point of the e-mail structure. This field describes the 'from' address of the e-mail. This specifies the sender's e-mail address.

  o **Date and time received (On:)**

  This part shows the date and time on which the message is received. This header section helps in tracing old or past e-mails.

  o **Reply-to**

  This field shows the e-mail address that will become the recipient of the reply to the particular e-mail. When you reply, it will go to this e-mail address despite the sender's e-mail address.

  o **Recipient (To:)**

  This header part is considered to be the destination point of the e-mail structure. This is the first/last name of the e-mail recipient as configured by the sender.

  o **Recipient e-mail address**

  The e-mail address of the recipient is specified here.

o **Forward**

This part is used to forward your e-mail to single or multiple recipients.

o **Attachments**

This part, as the name speaks for itself, is used to include some files as attachments such as texts, images, audios, videos, and so on.

- **Body**

The e-mail body is another vital sub-part of the e-mail structure. This part contains the actual content, either in a summarized or descriptive form. It includes simple text or multimedia text. It also includes signatures or text generated automatically by the sender's e-mail system. Depending upon the different e-mail systems used by each user, the contents of the email can vary.

3.5 E-mail delivery

E-mail delivery is the medium through which we can find out whether the sent e-mail has been delivered or not. It has the capacity to deliver the e-mail to the subscriber's inbox(es). E-mail marketers prefer to use this medium in computing the actual delivery of an e-mail in their subscriber's inboxes through the visualization of various parameters. The analysis of the parameters make a conclusive status as to whether the e-mail campaign has been successful or not. The parameters include various criteria such as actual delivery, timely delivery, bounce rate, spam issues, bulk, and so on. For example, if the delivery rate for your latest e-mail campaign is 89%, it means that your e-mails were delivered to 895 subscribers.

There are certain origins that harm the e-mail delivery rate. It is suggested to conduct a proper exercise in the e-mail delivery mechanism so that there is a minimal failure rate of deliverability. The origins that disturb deliverability include using short URLs, sending e-mails with multiple images, not properly providing the unsubscribe option, using a single opt-in medium, sending e-mail without custom authentication, and so on.

3.6 Offline and online data capture

There are two modes to capture data, namely online and offline. In the digital world, online marketing is on high priority but we cannot neglect offline marketing. Offline marketing has the aim of promoting businesses through trade shows and other mediums. Let's move ahead to understand more about both modes of data capturing procedures.

3.6.1 Collect database offline for e-mail marketing

In this section, the various stages related to database collection through offline mode are discussed.

- **From friends/relatives**

  The best way to gather data from friends and relatives is by sharing your thoughts honestly and telling them that you require their e-mail addresses and tell them about the offers in the form of products and services they will receive in return. For example, to promote goods such as electrical appliances, business owners collect the database in the offline mode through friends and their networks for e-mail marketing.

- **From colleagues**

  Another way to gather offline data for e-mail marketing is through colleagues. In any organization, your colleagues have their own friend circle or network who work in varying sectors depending on their job profiles. In a healthy and professional relationship, you can gather e-mail addresses of your colleague's friends or network.

- **Organize awareness campaigns**

  For business growth, plan and arrange awareness campaigns related to your products and services. Through these campaigns, there may be scope to reach the required segment of targeted consumers. For instance, you can conduct an awareness camp on the theme "How and where to purchase property?" To address all the relevant queries of the audience, you can have a platform of experts or counselors. During the campaign, with the help of the registration desk, you can collect the e-mail ids of all the visitors for future communication. This approach of data collection will help you in sharing your offers and other related information to your segment of customers in the nearby future.

- **Sponsor social events or organize your own event**

  An alternative way to gather data through the offline mode is to start participating in social events as a sponsor. For instance, join any social event like one for the World Yoga Day in which you can communicate to the organizer about your participation in the event as a sponsor and allow him to open a stall to promote his product and services. With this initiative, you may get the opportunity to retrieve the e-mail addresses of the interested visitors who might enroll themselves, and thus your objective will be achieved.

- **Tie up with corporate companies**

  Explore your area of connection with varying possibilities. Try to approach the company's key representative with your proposal to conduct some favorable events as per the interest of the audience once in a month. The events can be held on various themes such as entertainment, stress management, career counseling, and so on. During such an event, you may retrieve their comments in the form of a feedback form and further use them for e-mail marketing.

  To have a strong connection, be in touch with them some valuable association. For instance, every organization has some association. Now, this is the clicking moment of the marketer. You just have to tie up with the corporate companies and be a part of the program that they might do as an active member and start exploring your possibilities while having a connection with the audience and further get the relevant information. For example, if your target audience is women clients, then tie up with ladies clubs, kitty party clubs and so on. Alternatively, if you want to connect with medical doctors or physicians, then tie-up with a medical association.

3.6.2. Collect database online for e-mail marketing

In this section, the various operations related to database collection through the online mode will be discussed:

- **First, help them learn to trust you**

  According to expertise, "trust" is an important factor that makes you connect with the audience for a longer duration. The moment trust is gone; you will lose your targeted audience. To gain trust, the authenticity parameter of e-mail marketers should be high and in addition to this, they shouldserve their audience with the required content.

  To make your audience feel connected to you in an active manner, it is necessary that you gear them up regularly. While keeping regular touch with your targeted audience, help them in their relevant queries, and in return, ask them for additional details about them as per your interest to further utilize them in your respective personalized or customized activities.

- **Ask them to complete a sign-up form**

  Another approach in gathering online data is to ask the customer to fill a sign-up form. It is advisable that the sign-up form should be kept simple, clear, and precise. To keep an active connection with your targeted users, avoid framing a too long or complex-structured sign-up form.

  Through a customized sign-up form, it becomes a feasible to ask those questions of interest that are somehow not possible through the available tracking data. Also, it gives an opportunity to the user to label themselves as per their preference. Through a customized approach, there is always a scope of the probability of fetching the exact data of your interest from audiences in a friendly manner.

  Gathering online data through a sign-up form is a very important task. The objective of gathering data is to be very clear and focus. Do not collect data in a casual and unplanned way because this can act as a barrier when someone is first signing up. Also, asking for too many details can halt a potential user from signing up.

- **Make them an offer**

  Through e-mail marketing, there is always scope of connecting with audiences in a varying manner. People are generally interested in those initiatives which have some offers. It is natural that people proceed with those steps which have multiple benefits and provide savings in the packages of the offers. As a marketer, you should offer free stuff with your products and services so that audiences get connected to you instantly, and in return, they will often share their e-mail address or other additional details.

- **Survey them**

  The survey is one of the best mediums to know not only about the user interest but also about yourself as well as your organization. Through a survey form, you get the clear status about the customer's view towards your organization. With feedback, you can accordingly work on future market campaigns. For example, if the feedback is positive, you can take some more productive steps in the desired direction and if feedback is negative, you can take some preventive measures to improvise those things for the betterment and satisfaction of the customer.

  Surveys are a way through which you can gain a proper understanding of the behavior and interest of the user. Survey forms which are well managed help you in fetching some relevant details such as your customers' interest, their approach, what they think, what makes them more attracted or and what doesn't, and so on.

- **Invite them to compete for prizes**

  Organizing contests is a good practice for marketers. A contest organizing team that offers free of cost registration for participating as well as high chances of grabbing gifts will generally attract customers and they will willingly share their e-mail addresses and other details.

  There are various additional benefits in organizing contests such as growth in brand awareness, an increase in social media followers, extension in the lists of newsletter subscriptions, and help in driving customers to the websites.

3.7 Creating an e-mail campaign

Creating an e-mail campaign is a very challenging task. It all starts with proper planning, exercise, and execution. The basic steps for conducting an e-mail campaign in a strategic manner will help you in achieving your goal. So the general steps that are a part of the e-mail campaign which have to be followed before you hit the "send" button are as follows:

1. **Identify the need for an e-mail.**

   The initial step is to fetch the details regarding the need or requirement. Once that is gathered and understood, then only you can proceed to the next step.

2. **Document the campaign's requirements.**

   Proper documentation includes the source of information, its applicability, and its implementation which is then to be discussed and further formulated.

3. **Draft e-mail copy and find artwork.**

   Prefer including the artwork in the draft copy of the e-mail. The various sketches or pictures wherever required in the draft copy should be incorporated.

4. **Add copy and art to the template.**

   Always try to add the sample and drawing to the model or template. This practice helps in regaining the source information in a feasible manner.

5. **Set up tracking and add to the e-mail.**

   The tracking feature helps a lot in tracing your e-mail. This feature should be added in e-mail because it is the medium through which we can chase the movement of e-mail from source to destination.

6. **Test your e-mail and make edits.**

   E-mail testing should be done regularly. Also, whenever and wherever required, make necessary changes for the betterment of the e-mail framework and its related description.

7. **Complete the e-mail checklist.**

   A proper checklist should be maintained to be used as a repository for past, present as well as future e-mail proceedings.

8. **Send your e-mail.**

   Before sending your e-mail, it is a good practice to activate the "undo" feature through the settings option of e-mail. This activity helps you in previewing your details before finally sending it to the recipient.

   For instance, once you submit on the send button, a dialog box in the form of an alert message will appear as an "undo" option. If you feel that the mentioned description is okay in the e-mail, you can ignore the alert message and within a fraction of a second, it will disappear. In contradictory situations, if you notice some suspicious or missing element in the e-mail description, click on the alert message's "undo" option and your e-mail in the sending phase will be restored. Make some changes and then further resend your e-mail.

9. **Use data to revise tactics.**

Always prefer to use an alternative strategy to revise your text or multimedia description in the body section as well as the header section of your e-mail. Use the relevant data to fulfill the purpose.

3.8 Campaign measurement

To compute the efficiency of the campaign, most e-mail marketers offer some parameters. It is an easy task to trace and measure e-mail marketing. The main objective is to find those metrics that best evaluate your e-mail marketing. Here is a list of some vital metrics that will help you in evaluating the success of your e-mail marketing campaign.

1) **Deliverability**

It is one of the foremost metrics that help you in visualizing the performance. To conduct successful e-mail marketing, the deliverability status should be high. People will read an e-mail only if the corresponding e-mail is delivered to them without any delay or interruption.

2) **Open rates**

An open rate is another metric that gives a clear indication related to the success factor of your e-mail campaign. It gives you a signal about the applicability of your e-mail campaign. If your e-mail subject and description are being liked by the people, then they will be more willing to read and respond to your e-mails. This observation is computed in the form of the percentage of the number of people that open our emails which are referred to as open rates.

It is good practice to keep track of the different reactions of users. The average open rate count is 40%. Through open rate measurement, it can be analyzed what subject line attracts the customers most and in what frequency and duration.

3) Click-through rates

The click-through rate is another way to measure the appropriateness of the e-mail campaign. It measures what percentage of users clicks on the links shared in your e-mail. It highlights the measurement in the form of percentage which depicts the total number of e-mails opened.

To raise the percentage of the click-through rate, do your e-mail personalization in such a way that it will seem to the readers that the e-mail has been written in regards to them. You will get a better understanding of the preferences of users if you strongly observe which products and services your users click on.

4) Conversion rate

The conversion rate of e-mail marketing is measured with the help of web analytic tools. Through the conversion rate, you can get details that help in computing the financial success of the e-mail campaign.

It highlights how many users actually go from the e-mail to your website for product purchases. Moreover, it measures purchases in two ways, namely direct and indirect. This approach is computed on the criteria of whether the user approaches your website directly after being referred your offer through e-mail or some alternative or deviated path.

5) Bounce rate

Bounce rate refers to the status of those e-mails that are not delivered to the client's inbox, that is, they come back to the sender without reaching to the recipient. To determine the sender's credibility, the internet service provider plays a vital role in screening such type of bounce rates. There are two categories of bounce, namely soft bounce and hard bounce.

Soft bounce arises in a situation where your client's inbox is full. Although some servers will try to resend soft bounce e-mails at a later phase, it is suggested that you note such type of soft bounces to be included in the category of "resend the e-mail" in the next campaign. A hard bounce arises in a situation where the recipient's e-mail address is not valid or does not exist. In such type of circumstance, it is advised that you should not maintain a hard bounce list because it will affect your sender's credibility. As per a study, it has been stated to clear your mail listings after each campaign.

6) **Unsubscribe rate**

This reflects the ratio of clients who are not attached or connected with your agenda or the description mentioned in your e-mails. As per experts, it has been declared that 2% of unsubscribe rate is acceptable. If the percentage of unsubscribe rate is more than 2%, it means that you have to work on your marketing strategies more. The best practice is that you should be in contact with your clients regularly while sharing your e-mails with them so that the gap between you and your clients remains minimal or negligible.

7) **Abuse reports**

This refers to those cases where the subscriber marks your e-mail as spam and it reflects in your abuse report count. It happens in a situation where the subscriber instead of opening an e-mail and clicking on the unsubscribe link, marks your e-mail as spam. They do this type of activity because they find it to be an easier way of ignoring an e-mail that is not of their interest.

Although your e-mail service provider will alert you if there is an increase in the number of abuse reports, it is suggested that you keep track of abuse reports on your account on a regular basis. This type of situation should be avoided because it is actually a spam complaint that goes directly to your client's internet service provider and hence will block all the e-mails sent from your e-mail address.

8) **Revenue**

Revenue is the most important measure of success for online businesses. It is very important to keep track of your e-mail return on investment. The objective of successful e-mail marketing is not just to stay in touch with your clients but also to generate direct sales. It is a good practice to use the Google analytic tools to compute the revenue generation from the e-mail marketing campaign.

3.9 Concept of A/B testing and its use in e-mail marketing

A/B testing is a concept that is used to test your e-mail campaigns. This testing is applied on two options named as version 'A' and version 'B' and further testing is done on both options in evaluating their effectiveness. The computation of both options is done on the basis of the numbers of click parameter. This testing is also known as split testing.

The working of A/B testing starts with the setup process of two versions for one e-mail campaign. Initially, a small percentage of your total recipients will be shared equally in both versions, that is, half of them will be sent to version 'A' and the other half will be sent to version 'B'. After computation, the result will be measured on the basis of the maximum number of clicks. On comparative studying, the version achieving the maximum clicks will be considered as the winning version which will be further sent to the remaining subscribers. When an A/B testing is in process, you cannot change the campaign, but you can cancel it before it is sent to the entire list.

Categories of A/B testing

There are some categories of A/B testing which help in the process of testing to find the winning version of the e-mail campaign for further proceedings.

1) **Subject line**

    The subject line is one of the types of A/B testing which helps in achieving the winning result from the two set up versions of the testing procedure. Both versions, 'A' and 'B,' are identical except the subject line which is the main source of A/B testing for doing a comparative study. For example, you could test the generic subject lines and long subject lines through A/B testing. It is not necessary that the generic subject line will get more number of clicks in comparison to the long subject line. It all depends upon the content writing, situation, demand, and interest of the client.

    Another way of doing A/B testing is to test two completely different topics as the subject line. After the completion of A/B testing, you can analyze which text or content is most opened or clicked by subscribers. You can also do an A/B testing test by including different offers in the identical subject line. For instance, different offers such as "20% off" versus "free shipping" can be used for testing purposes.

    You can also personalize with the same subject line to check which version gets the winning response. For example, as shown in *Figure 3.1*, you can perform A/B testing by checking if the first name greeting in version 'B' gets a more winning response in comparison to the non-greeting approach in version 'A.'

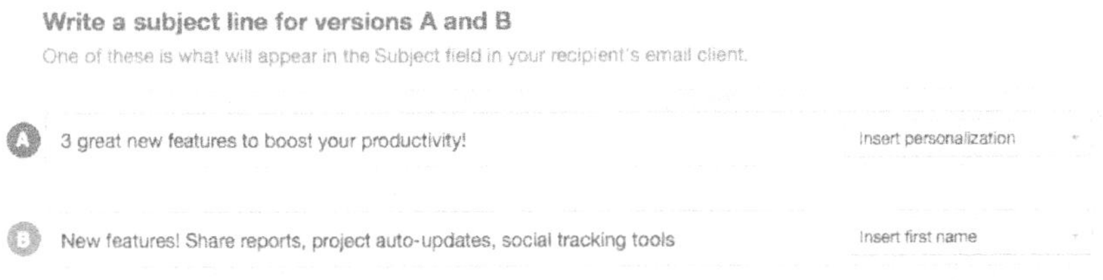

Write a subject line for versions A and B
One of these is what will appear in the Subject field in your recipient's email client.

(A)   3 great new features to boost your productivity!   Insert personalization

(B)   New features! Share reports, project auto-updates, social tracking tools   Insert first name

Figure 3.1: *Concept of subject line*

2) From name

"From name" means sender details. It is important to mention the sender details as it helps the client or user in recognizing the e-mail. Many users avoid opening an e-mail that does not have proper details. With the "Form name" type of testing, you can use different names and e-mail addresses for version 'A' and version 'B' as shown in *Figure 3.2*. The best practice depends on how well you are connected with your subscriber. Some clients are likely to remember or connect via company name, individual name, or product name.

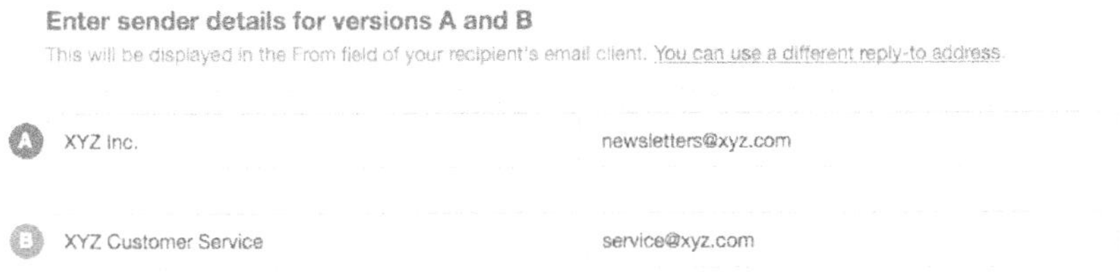

Enter sender details for versions A and B
This will be displayed in the From field of your recipient's email client. You can use a different reply-to address.

(A)   XYZ Inc.   newsletters@xyz.com

(B)   XYZ Customer Service   service@xyz.com

Figure 3.2: *Concept of sender details*

3) E-mail content

This type of testing is applicable to various elements of e-mails such as header images, article length, section, and so on. You can perform A/B testing in two different designs to see which one receives the maximum number of clicks. This type of test can be built using one of the designed, automated, or saved templates. To apply testing on the "e-mail content" type, follow the instructions to set up version 'A' first. Once it is complete, apply the same procedure to version 'B'. The structure of the e-mail content is demonstrated in *Figure 3.3* with the applicability of various stages of testing.

Figure 3.3: Layout of e-mail content

If you are use the same template with minor changes in the content, then you can save your time and effort by copying the content from version 'A' to create version 'B'. You can do this by selecting your content of version 'A' from the top left corner of the template library tab Recent e-mails as shown in *Figure 3.4.*

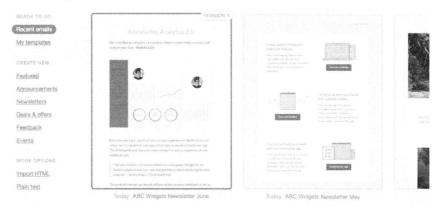

Figure 3.4: An approach of recent e-mail activity

4) Choose recipients

You will be prompted to choose the subscriber list when both versions of the campaign are established. Once the A/B test has started, no other subscriber list can be entertained. If there is a need to consider a new subscriber list, then it will be accepted separately for the alternative test.

5) Define test settings

The A/B testing is performed with some settings such as selecting the size of the test group, test duration, and on what parameters the winner will be chosen.

6) **Test group size**

The size of the test group has to be pre-decided, that is, decided before starting the test. Generally, a small subset of your recipients having a slide of 20-30% is preferred. The selection of recipients is done on a random basis from the test group. On selection, half of them will be sent to version 'A' and the other half will be sent to version 'B'. The remaining recipients will be sent to the winning version.

3.10 Digital display advertising - concepts, benefits, and challenges

Digital display advertising, as the name suggests, is used for banner advertisement on various social media platform such as Facebook, Twitter, and so on. It comes in different forms it resolves around the same principle but at its core.

3.10.1 Concepts

Display advertising is one of the frequently used approaches in digital marketing. It highlights the commercial message visually using text, audio, video, images, logos, and graphics. Its objective is to regularly connect with target users with the makeup of the necessary particulars published in digital advertisements which are related to the product and services.

3.10.2 Benefits

Digital display advertising has many benefits that help in improvising your business. The main objective is to hold your audience so that you can decide where to reach them online.

- **Effective targeting**

  Effective targeting through display advertising can be achieved in four different manners. The aim is to highlight your brand and online visibility with your advertisements so as to reach to wider and unique audiences in a potential way.

- **Remarketing**

  Remarketing is one of the concepts of effective marketing that works on connecting with those clients who show interest in your business or products through website s or mobile app visits. This is also known as **retargeting** as it provides you the possibility to highlight your advertisements to the clients who have previously visited your online platform. For instance, AdWords drive your clients to your respective online platform when they are most engaged which is one of the best instances of remarketing.

- **Audience targeting**

  Its focus is to reach the audience through your online advertisements in varying modes. While following the principle of effective marketing, it allows you to reach the audiences who have an interest in the products and services that are similar to your business's products. It gives you the possibility of using ad groups based on your advertising objective to showcase your products with an interest in certain categories or offers on the relevant websites or apps.

- **Demographic targeting**

  This medium of effective targeting provides you with an opportunity to choose clients based on particular demographic classifications such as gender, age range, region, and so on. There is a flexibility to exclude certain types of demographic groupings to prevent them from seeing your advertisements.

- **Customer match**

  This mode of effective targeting helps you in representing your advertisements to customers on different social platforms like Google search, YouTube, and Gmail using details of those customers that you share with Google.

- **Flexible cost**

  The payment mode of your digital display advertising is flexible. There are two options for payment, namely **cost per click (CPC)** and **cost per thousand impressions (CPM).** In CPC, you will be charged for each click on your advertisements. It is the most widely used option and in CPM, you will be charged based on the number of impressions your advertisements receive.

  The flexible cost is applicable in the manner that you set the price of the advertisements that you want to pay for. Once your advertisement is displayed, it will go into the auction and your advertisement price will be compared with the other advertiser's set prices. In the final auction, whosoever loses the bid announces a winner and finally gets the advertisement spot.

- **Measure results**

  The major benefit of digital display advertising is that you have the ability to monitor your advertisement, that is, you can check the frequency of clicks on your advertisement. In addition to this, you can receive daily or weekly reports related to your advertisement response on a digital platform. The web analytic tools help you in accessing the information regarding whether your advertisement is performable or not. If it is acting well, then it is good, otherwise you need to rework your efforts. The tracking tools help you in gathering reports on your website traffic, brand awareness, sales, and conversion.

  Measuring results provide you with a clear understanding and analysis of whether you have chosen the right keywords and segmented the clients list properly or not. If your advertisement is missing your target audience, then it means that your advertisements are being seen by the wrong audience. In other words, you are far from your potential clients.

3.10.3 Challenges and solutions

Besides benefits, there are some challenges of digital display advertising which we will learn in this section.

Challenge 1: To make sure that your advertisements appear in the appropriate places on the digital platform.

It is a very challenging activity to ensure the right placement of your advertisements on the web. The solution to overcome this challenge is to give more attention to your advertisements for at least 20 minutes on a day-to-day basis. Maintain the placement of your advertisements where the response rate is in your favor, and if the situation is just the opposite, remove those that do not make sense. Either follow an automatic process that is less time-consuming or proceed with a manual process which is more time-consuming for the right engagement of your advertisements on the web.

Challenge 2: To ensure that advertisement impressions are seen in a decent manner.

It is a challenging part to validate the maximum observance of advertisement impressions. As per a study, it came to notice that 56% of advertisements' impressions are not noticed. The solution to defeating this challenge is to retarget campaigns and formulate custom segmentation. Both approaches are to be proceeded with while keeping the point of view of the right content in the right place. Through the approach of retargeting, you can build up the list of custom segmentation on the basis of demographic, content-specific, and the nature of users. This activity will help you in marketing or displaying content to those clients who have previously have been attached to your business proposals.

Challenge 3: To defeat the situation of banner blindness

As per a recent study, it came to notice that the percentage of banner blindness is severely increased in display advertising which is a threat alarm to digital marketers. The solution to conquer this challenge is to stay on the top and follow the best practices in your organization. Also, a Google study states that view ability rates vary across content, location, and demographic conditions. Also, page position is not the best sign of view ability. It depends on the phenomena of marketing strategies, that is, to work on the engagement of the right audiences with the right content and right placements.

Challenge 4: To manage unnecessary impressions of advertisements

In some situations, it came to notice that impressions point in the range of hundreds to thousands in just a single day. This may happen due to some breaking news or sensational activity that may cause your advertisement to display more than its normal frequency. This effects badly in terms of increased cost and reduces **click-through rate (CTR)**. The solution to overcome this challenge is to not fixed your advertisement and forget it. Keep your eye on the reactions of display advertisements and ensure the maintenance and health of your overall account.

Challenge 5: To maintain consistency across channels with display advertisements

It is a challenging task to incorporate your display advertisements with other channels. The solution to overcome this challenge is to promote trade shows through display advertisements. This approach is known as a cross channel marketing strategy. Thisd helps in maintaining the consistency and development of your brand while enhancing results from display advertisements. With this approach, the users not only see your advertisements but they will visit your page and you will further retrieve the relevant content as per your interests.

3.11 Ad formats

Ad formats refer to those creative approaches which help you in achieving your potential customers.

1) **Targeted advertising**

   To explore your digital advertising campaign, an automated ad format plays a very important role. Through the programming techniques and animated embedded appearance, it allows marketers to cover the overall client experience across all expected outcomes. With these creative initiatives, your brand gets an opportunity to highlight their picture in an engaging and fruitful manner. So, ad formats based on targeted advertising help in reaching your clients more effectively and further converting your clients into a higher return on investment.

2) Maximum monetization

To achieve maximum monetization, smart ads show their real involvement in varying ways. With the smart ads format, the publisher can do a comparative study with existing and potential ads. This study helps in drawing a conclusion to select the creative ad that best connects with the audiences. To deliver rich client experiences, app developers work on choosing many ad types of varying sizes that are fully compatible across screens. Multiple web analytics tools allow you to provide results based on tracking the performance of a similar pattern of ads so that you can prepare a well-optimized and efficient ad as per the demand.

3.12 Ad features

Ad features discuss interactive communication, a result-oriented approach, and focus on the targeted audience, and how exactly digital marketing helps in establishing a business.

1. Audience reach out

This is one of the prime objectives of digital marketers, that is, how to reach the audience in an efficient and effective manner. The content in the advertisement should be framed in a creative and visualized manner. Once developed, it is further widely promoted over social media channels in which buyers can access information about the company's product and services. This practice will motivate buyers to share their experience with their peer group or network.

Digital marketers supersede traditional marketers as they can approach clients at any time with minimal effort. They do not require reaching customers through unnecessary and consistent phone calls which is considered to be an outdated approach nowadays. For example, a digital marketer simply sends an e-mail to their potential or targeted customers while offering them some discount or offer on purchasing their products.

2. Interactive communication

Interactive communication is possible in the digital marketing world through feedback. It is the medium through which users can interact with the companies about their corresponding goods through an online platform. They are considered to be a strong contributor to branding and the offering of goods. In today's scenario, with the support of easy-to-use online tools, it becomes a comfortable way for the organization to take online feedback from users. This feedback helps companies in retrieving the information that reflects the buying behavior of the user as well as their reactions towards their goods and services. Thus, companies can alter the product offerings and market communication based on user requirement, response, and satisfaction.

3. **Result-oriented approach**

A competitive environment creates a result-oriented approach. There is always competition in business as well as in a market where one company works closely with another company to defeat each other and move ahead.

Search engine optimization is a digital marketing technique that helps in navigating priority-based proposed traffic to your online platform. These type of advanced marketing strategies are capable of improving your web page ranking which makes them capable of being listed at the top of the **search engine result page (SERP)**. It is one of the ways which justifies the result-oriented approach in a competitive business environment.

Another popular strategy is **conversion rate optimization (CRO)**. It helps in targeting those audiences which exhibit more potential in conversion rate, that is, high probability in becoming a customer. These outcomes support digital marketers in understanding whether they are targeting the right kind of traffic or not.

4. **Focused audience targeting**

Digital marketing has a wider scope of reaching the audience. It is not restricted to targeting a small group of audience. It is flexible enough to expand its strategy to reach out to a wider range of audiences and highlight the brand, product, and services on digital media, e-mails, websites, and so on.

It applies varying strategies for the involvement of targeting audiences. These techniques help in engaging audiences towards their products. So, targeting online users and converting the incoming web traffic into leads is the prime objective of digital marketing strategies. Alternative strategies that are used to draw the kind intention of potential users into conversion ratios are inventory targeting and user targeting.

In inventory marketing, advertisements with specific content are offered by marketers to promote their brands which are visited by users in one particular demographic whereas user targeting focuses on only those users who show specific attention towards the marketer's interest.

3.13 Ad display frequency

Ad display frequency is one of the important mediums to check the success rate of marketing campaigns. The best way is to calculate the effective frequency for your advertisements. Effective frequency means the number of times that users are shown your advertising message. To put it simply, the presence of a user for viewing a particular advertisement related to buying a product or service does not mean that the deal is done. There is another possibility that the user just remembers that advertising message.

So, to know about the actual status in terms of "effective frequency," it is necessary to determine your return on investment. For example, many marketers believe that if consumers see your advertisements more than seven times, then there will be a high chance they will become your potential customer, that is, the product will be purchased by the client. But such type of a belief is not the exact criteria to determine the effective frequency of advertisements. There may be some exceptions where clients make a deal with less than seven visits to your advertisement.

With such a hypothetical situation, let's take the following factors into consideration to better understand how a small-medium enterprise identifies the effective frequency of advertisements.

Factor 1: How established is the brand?

There is no doubt in saying that mature or established brands will receive more desirable customers in comparison to newly entrant organizations. Startup companies need to spend more time in analysis to identify their potential customers according to their brand and products.

Factor 2: Who is the target demographic?

The second most valuable factor is to determine target audiences based on demographic criteria. It is vital to identify the categories of clients. The more you know about your audience, the better you will be able to decide the most effective frequency. For instance, if you are offering cartoon movie content in your advertisement then in that case, teenagers will see your ad more times in comparison to another age group.

Factor 3: What is the overall objective of your ad?

This factor states your goal for your advertisement. Each advertisement campaign should have a clear aim. On the basis of a clear objective, it will be easier to retrieve your desired customers and further come up with the evaluation of the right frequency.

Factor 4: Market saturation

Market saturation is a challenging factor of the digital advertising campaign. The more saturated your market is, the more efforts you have to make to drive your audiences towards your advertisement. The best way is to increase the number of your display advertisements so that your clients remember your brand for further proceedings.

Factor 5: Is the purchase big or small?

This factor highlights the topic of how much money is to be spent in your advertisement. This is a hypothetical question. The answer to this key question varies from case to case. For instance, if you are selling pizza, expect to run your advertisements more than if you were selling a pen. The approach of effective frequency in terms of "big or small" criteria is based on various parameters such as type of organization, date of establishment of the company, type of product, its price, volume, budget of marketing, and so on. All these highlighted parameters will help in the decision-making process to proceed to the step of running an advertisement in an effective manner.

3.14 Overview of Google AdWords

Google AdWords is a digital platform that followed by any marketer to explore their business from a new height of success and brand awareness. It is the medium through which companies pay to have their website ranked high in the top search list based on keywords.

A keyword is a word or phrase that is associated with your advertisements. The user searches for the keyword and then sees your advertisement. Your advertisement will be displayed on the basis of the keywords you pick.

Google computes the **click-through rate (CTR)** on the basis of the number of clicks and impressions. CTR is the percentage of users who land on your advertised page. If you divide the number of clicks by impressions, you will get the result in the form of CTR. Also, counts are computed by Google on a chargeable basis, that is, Google charges you for each click on your advertisement. Similarly, Google also counts impressions which state how often your advertisements were shown when the user searched for the keyword that you mentioned. *Figure 3.5* demonstrates the layout of Google AdWords.

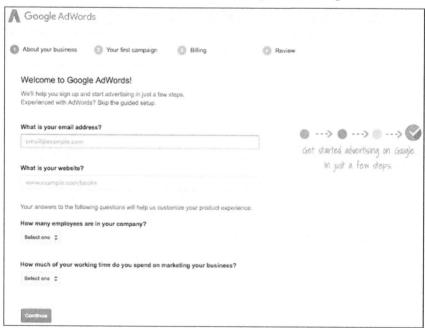

Figure 3.5: Layout of Google AdWords

Google AdWords is an auction house where you set a budget and bid. The bid value states the amount that you are willing to pay per click. Google will show your advertisement to audiences on the basis of the maximum bid or computation of average bidding by other bidders. Google does not believe in showing the advertisement to people having the highest bid. Instead, it cares about their users and shows them relevant and better advertisements, no matter whether or not the bid value is low. Hence, Google's center of attention is to win on the basis of quality advertisements and good bids.

Create a Google AdWords account

To create a Google AdWords account, visit **https://www.adwords. google.com/**. From there, you can create your account and set up your first campaign. Here are the steps:

1. Select your campaign type and name.

2. Choose the geographic location where you'd like the ads to be shown.

3. Choose your "bid strategy" and set your daily budget. Change the default "Bid strategy" to "I will manually set my bids for clicks." This gives you more control and will help you learn AdWords with a greater level of understanding.

4. Create your first ad group and write your first ad. More people click on ads when the headline includes the keyword that they are searching. So use your keywords in your headlines whenever you can. You are limited to 25 characters here so for some search terms, you'll need to use abbreviations or shorter synonyms. Here is the short version of your ad template:

   o **Headline:** Up to 25 characters of text

   o **2nd line:** Up to 35 characters

   o **3rd line:** Up to 35 characters

   o **4th line:** Your display URL

5. Insert your keywords into the keyword field in your account. Paste your keywords. Start with just one set and add plus signs (+), brackets ([ ]), and quotes (" ") to see precisely how many searches of each type you get.

6. Set your maximum cost per click. Set your maximum price per click (called your "default bid"). However, realize that every keyword is theoretically a different market which

means that each of your major keywords will need a bid price of its own. Google will let you set individual bids for each keyword later.

7. Enter your billing information.

Conclusion

In this chapter, we have discussed the concept of e-mail marketing and its applicability in e-mail list generation, structure, and delivery. We also had a walkthrough on creating an email campaign and its measurement. We discussed the concept of A/B testing and its use in e-mail marketing. Additionally, we highlighted the concepts, benefits, and challenges of digital display advertising.

In the next chapter, we will see an overview of social media marketing.

Points to remember

- An e-mail has three basic parts. The message itself is made up of the two following elements: the header fields and a set of lines describing the message's settings such as the sender, recipient, date, and so on.

- E-mail deliverability is the ability to deliver e-mails to the subscribers' inboxes.

- E-mail marketing is easy to track and measure. Most e-mail marketing platforms offer hosts of data that help you to measure the efficiency of your e-mail campaigns. Your task is to find those metrics such as deliverability, open rates, click-through rates, conversion rates, and bounce rates that best suit your e-mail marketing goals and to keep an eye on them.

- A/B testing, also known as split testing, is a way of working out which of two campaign options is the most effective in terms of encouraging opens or clicks.

MCQs

1. **Which of the following comes under e-mail marketing?**

   a) E-mail newsletters

   b) Lead nurturing

   c) Digests

   d) All of the above

2. **Which of the following is the most important metric to track e-mail marketing?**

    a) CTR

    b) Open rate

    c) Click rate

    d) All of the above

3. **How important is the authentication process in e-mail marketing?**

    a) Not important

    b) Can be skipped

    c) Very important

    d) Depends on the individual

4. **In which type of e-mail campaign, advertisements are sent to the target group of customers?**

    a) Direct email marketing

    b) Indirect email marketing

    c) Spamming

    d) Spoofing

5. **Which of the following is the correct size of an e-mail template before executing a campaign?**

    a) 15 KB

    b) 18 KB

    c) 20 KB

    d) 15 MB

Answers

1. *d*
2. *d*
3. *c*
4. *a*
5. *b*

Questions

1. What's the point of e-mail marketing?

2. How do I grow my e-mail subscriber list?

3. What are the best practices for e-mail subject lines?

4. What are the laws of e-mail marketing?

5. What other metrics should I track for e-mail marketing?

Key terms

E-mail marketing: Email marketing is all about assumption and it's up to you to place them. It allows business representatives to approach past and new customers, present themselves formally to the current as well as future prospects regarding the products and their related offers.

CHAPTER 4
Social Media Marketing

Social media marketing is now a proven way for companies to reach new customers, interact with old customers, and encourage their tone, mission, or culture. Also termed as "e-marketing" and "digital marketing," marketing on social media has tools that are used to analyze data and allow marketers to track how successfully their strategies are performing. What's the impact of social media on search engine optimization? What are the basic approaches to social media marketing? How to create and test landing pages? You will find the answer to these questions in this chapter and the subsequent ones. So let's get started!

Structure

In this chapter, we will cover the following topics:

4.1 Key concepts of social media marketing

4.2 Different social media channels: Facebook, Twitter, and YouTube

4.3 Business page: setup and profile

4.4 Social media content

Objective

After studying this chapter, you should be able to:

- Understand the importance of social media marketing.
- Understand the concepts of CPC, PPC, CPM, CTR, and CPA.
- Remember various multimedia elements.

4.1 Key concepts of social media marketing

Social media marketing is generally termed as the process of gaining the visitors' attention from different social media platforms such as Facebook, Instagram, LinkedIn, and so on. Social media is a very catchy name for sites in itself that may invoke some different social actions. For example, social sites like Twitter are developed to allow users to share short messages or "updates" with their friends, family, and other users.

Social media sometimes lets the users to the discovery of new things like news stories, and "discovery" is a search page area of social media platforms. **Search engine optimization (SEO)** efforts can also be made more effective by building links from social media that in turn build more support. Many users make searches in social media platforms also in order to find the social media content that they want or are interested in. Sometimes, your connections on social media sites may also affect the relevancy of some results of the searched query, either within a social media platform or in some major search engine.

4.2 Different social media channels – Facebook, Twitter, and YouTube

There are different social media channels that are available in the digital world. From the long list of channels, let's have a brief discussion on Facebook, Twitter, and YouTube.

Facebook

With over 1.6 billion active users every single month, Facebook is one of the most popular as well as the most important platform, not only for users to just share their personal stuff but for the business as well. For businesses, Facebook is a platform where you can share general news, updates, and photos with those who are interested, like, or follow your business or are related to it. Followers of your business can come to your Facebook page to know about the events that are going on in the company and see pictures of your new products or your new services.

How to use Facebook for marketing?

Firstly, you have to start getting followers on Facebook. You have to make your page a public page (that everyone can reach out to), share a link of it wherever you can, and add all social sites icons onto your website.

When you have created a huge fan-base, it is necessary to update your status or photos to allow your followers to share your offers, services, and products. You also have to post things that engage your followers such as posts that they may like, share, and comment on. The more people that engage, the more chances are that you will appear in their timelines.

It is necessary to keep in mind that most of the users use Facebook as a personal network to get in touch with their relatives, friends, or loved ones. So, you have to fit into that ecosystem to keep people liking and interested in your brand's posts. So make sure that you don't make that account solely about selling.

Tool to utilize – Advertising

Facebook Advertising is the highest in-demand tool in the current business world and it is growing at a tremendous speed.

In this, social media activities are used to point out those who come under your buyer demographics in order to make Facebook advertisements (ads) more and more effective. Facebook ads have more potential of bringing in buyers or strong leads that are really looking for services like yours.

Twitter

Twitter is a concise, fast-paced, and easy method to connect with your audience. It currently has more than 310 million users (and growing). Twitter is an ocean of information where content of 140 characters or less is read, re-tweeted, followed, and clicked on.

How to use Twitter for marketing?

On Twitter, more than 175 million tweets are generated on a daily basis and let you share quick information and photos by which you can drive people (back) to your business site, target pages, or landing pages. You get very less amount of characters for this, so use them wisely.

While using Twitter for marketing, you must have content that is very attractive for people that stop them and they click through it. People generally scroll quickly so it needs more than just some piece of text to stop them in their work or scrolling. Make sure enough when you are making your tweets that your goal is to make people click through your tweets. Try to use questions, statistics, quotes, or links related to your tweet by which people want more to read. Incorporate short videos, gifs, polls, or photos.

While Twitter is an extraordinary method to share brisk considerations and redirect traffic to your site and offers, it is imperative to ensure you are additionally maintaining a relationship with your followers.

Users follow you because they like what you have got to mention, but often also to interact in conversation. Like you do on Facebook, ask and answer questions, answer mentions, and direct messages. Twitter is as useful for both driving traffic and customer service.

Tool to utilize: Hashtags

Hashtags (#) are the main tool to use on Twitter. These hashtags will allow you to reach a huge user base instead of just your followers by letting them get involved in existing conversations.

It is seen on Twitter that users searching for a particular piece of information will often look at hashtags to see what is out there. Do some research about what kind of hashtags your buyer is using to make sure your posts will be found by the right user base.

YouTube

YouTube is now becoming the world leader across all video sharing platforms in the world. On your brand's YouTube channel, you can edit and share your own videos, create playlists, and start discussions. YouTube is one of the platforms that the search engines give importance to in the search results page so take full advantage of it.

How to use YouTube for marketing?

For your business, YouTube an be a great way to create more and more awareness about your brand in your industry. Studies have shown that videos get more engagement and are share more than textual content and they also support your search rank in **search engine result page (SERP)**. When creating video content for YouTube, you must consider quality as the main factor. Before uploading any content, make sure there is a well-defined purpose and you have given value to what you are uploading. Also, make sure to pay attention to your production values. Both the audio and video of the content that you are uploading should be very clear, crisp, and easy to understand. There should be no blurriness or shaky cameras.

Tool to utilize: YouTube Studio

YouTube Studio is like a new home for YouTube creators. By using this, you can manage your business' YouTube channel and get insights. It also lets you stay updated with the latest news about YouTube's new rules and regulations. YouTube Studio has replaced the old creator studio classic and brings with it many updates and new features that will enhance your productivity.

4.3 Business page: setup and profile

In today's scenario, a business page is a necessary requirement. To explore your business in the digital world, setting up a business page and profile is mandatory. Here are the steps that will guide you:

Step 1: Sign up

The first step regarding the setup of a business page is to create a page on Facebook. In this section, you will observe different types of business categories of choices such as brand details, location, and source of information. After that, you will select the type of business. The business type reflects the theme of your business page creation. As per expert suggestion, if your business type falls under more than two categories, you have to make the decision of choosing one out of the other options on the basis of the targeted customer's interest.

Once you click on the business type, a dialog box will open in which you have to fill details such as business name, address, and page category. There a list of potential category options from which you can choose your preferred category type. Basically, there are various options that come under the umbrella of a larger business category that you have already selected from the specific list. *Figure 4.1* demonstrates the signup page for a business setup or profile in which you can mention your particulars like name of the business, address, contact details, and so on.

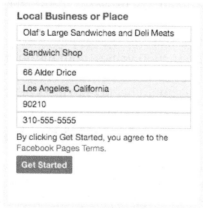

Figure 4.1: Screenshot of Get Started

Once all the relevant details have been filled by you in your respective business page, click on **Get Started**. Doing this means that you have accepted the terms and conditions for a business page on Facebook. It is advised to make sure that you carefully observe all the activities properly before proceeding further.

Step 2: Add pictures

This step focuses on adding a picture to your Facebook business page. For this, you have to upload a profile picture and cover images. It is very important to pay proper attention to the picture inclusion task. It is suggested that the image should be chosen in such a manner that it correlates with your brand and can be easily recognized with respect to your business.

Now, the initial step is to upload your profile picture. The purpose of the profile picture is to make your communication most effective with your users. To fulfill this goal, the image must assist the name of your business in search results. There are various cases that highlight the different possibilities of connecting with your customer through your profile picture. If you are a public figure, your own picture will work perfectly. In another case, if you are brand and have a logo, then it is likely the best way to go ahead, or if you have a local business, a well-shot image of your signature will be the best way to allow users to make the connection with you instantly.

In your business page, it has been said that your profile picture will appear as a square on your Facebook page but will appear in a circular shape in advertisements and posts, so do not put any key or main details in the corner of the image. Once you have completed this, click on **Upload Profile Picture**.

The next step is to choose the cover image for your business page. The cover page also reflects your business persona. Make sure that you select the cover image that reflects the crux of your brand and highlights it in a very forwarding approach. There are different dimensions of cover images. Once you have chosen an appropriate image for the cover image, click on **Upload a Cover Photo**.

Step 3: Explore your new page

At this stage, you will be taken to a quick walk-through of a few options or features that you will have. If you are not familiar with how Facebook Business pages really work, then we suggest that you click on all the prompts that appear one by one, just so you know where everything is. It takes very less amount of time to go through all of this. *Figure 4.2* highlights the screenshot that discusses exploring a new page.

Figure 4.2: Screenshot of exploring new page

So, the structure of your Facebook business page is now completed. But you still have to do some work before you can share it with the public or your audience.

Step 4: Add a short description

This is the opportunity that you have to grab and wisely utilize to tell the audience about your business. There should not be bulky information. It must be a couple of sentences (maximum 155 characters), so you need not elaborate much here. Click on add a **short description** and then just write what you think your customers want and need to know but in a clear and concise manner.

You can also write a longer description later on if you want to. *Figure 4.3* demonstrates adding a short description of your business.

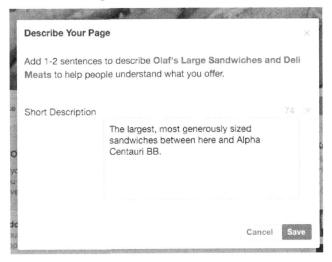

Figure 4.3: Screenshot to add a short description

Click on **Save** when you are done.

Step 5: Create your username

Your vanity URL, also called your username, is that by which users will find you and your business on Facebook. It can be up to 50 characters long but we strongly recommend that you not use mush characters. You have to make it easy to remember and easy to type. It is recommended that usernames should contain the name of your business or some obvious variation to keep it simple. *Figure 4.4* highlights the description regarding creating page username.

Figure 4.4: Screenshot of creating a page username

Click on **Create Username** when you have chosen your username. Then, a dialog box will pop up that will show you the links that users can use to reach your business on Facebook and Facebook messenger. *Figure 4.5* shows the acknowledgment related to the creation of a username.

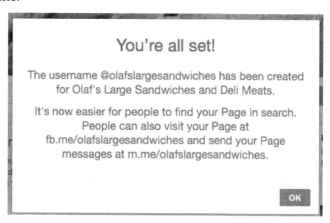

Figure 4.5: Layout of creation of a username

On **OK** to continue filling in your Facebook business page details.

Step 6: Complete your about section

It is important and valuable to fill all the fields on your Facebook business page. The 'About' section includes some information that basically highlights your business page and makes it more informative and attractive. Facebook is a popular platform where the user often visits to gather information about you. For instance, if someone is looking for a business and is unable to find the information on your page, then they will surely explore some alternative which may be another place.

The best practice that is to be followed is to highlight the information about your Facebook messenger protocol. It includes facilities like online customer service response hours and an estimated time of response.

To proceed further, click on the **About** section on the top left side of your Facebook page. In this section, you can add or edit business-related information such as business details, start date, business types, contact information, e-mail, website details, and other account details. Additionally, you can add specific details like the price range of products and some promotional offers.

There is one important part of the **About** section in which you can share a longer description of your business. Just click on **Edit story** and you will be able to write your description. This page description helps customers in understanding your business-related background details and their expectations towards your business increases by reading this section. This is a nice section where you can interact with your fans or followers for business purposes and also offer them an attentive reason for them to engage with you online. When you are finished, click on **Save Changes**. *Figure 4.6* shows the page of the **About** section and its importance.

Figure 4.6: Screenshot of the About section

Step 7. Create your first post

When you create your first post, make sure that you share some valuable content. You can create some of your own posts or share some relevant information from thought leaders of your industry.

You could also create a post of some contest, event, or product offer. Once you are prepared, just click through the tabs at the top of the status box to bring up all the options.

Step 8: Start engaging

At this final step, you are ready to invite your family and friends to like the page. At this point, you are in a position to give your Facebook business page a bit of change. Use your alternative medium like your website or other social media channels to promote your business page. Add the "follow us" logo on your promotional campaigns and e-mail signature. Also, ask your customers to give their reviews on your Facebook business page.

4.4 Social media content

Social media content can also be referred to as interactive media as it highlights products and services on the digital system which further proceed in responding to the user's action by communicative mediums such as text, audio, video, image, and animation.

Infographics

Infographics may be defined as visual representation of information or data. In other words, they refer to the collection of images, charts, graphs, and minimal text. They are one of the most widely used social media content. They have a huge impact on presentations and documents.

Interactive content

Interactive content is the next popular form of social media content. Through this form, it becomes easier to answer the user's query on the digital platform. Texts, moving images, videos, audios, gamess, and so on are the example of interactive content.

Content that involves strong positive emotion

Social media content has beautiful characteristics of involvement. It gets connected with audiences through emotional value. Sharing posts on social media platforms in done in such a manner that it evokes positive emotion which makes audiences get connected in a frequent and active manner.

Content with images

For effective reach to the audiences on social media platforms, content with images play a very important role. It is confirmed from advisors that image-rich content is highly shareable. *Figure 4.7* shows the comparative study of tweet analysis in which, as per the analytical study, it came to be known that tweets with images have better performance than tweets without images.

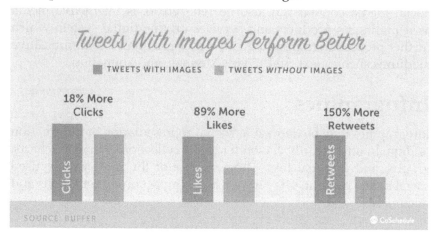

Figure 4.7: Tweets analysis with images and without images

List posts

To raise the number of social shares, a list post is the right approach. Next to infographics, it is considered to be the most popular format. Users love to share lists and infographics. It lists a number of tips, methods, shortcuts, secrets, types, ways, trends, and many more things.

4.5 Impact of Social Media on SEO

There is a huge impact of social media on search engine optimization (SEO). There are various reasons for that such as that social sharing leads to traffic, raises the profile rank, improves your content reach, uplifts brand awareness, and many more. Let us consider six ways in which social media impacts SEO:

Social sharing drives traffic to websites

Sharing of posts in social media platforms that consist of quality content can gather likes, comments, and shares. This also motivates social media users to move to official business websites.

To keep your brand in a high list, it is advised to keep your potential customers in an engaging mode. You can increase your natural search ranking by pulling your social web traffic back to the official business website. This provides high authority to your site in the observance of search engines.

Note: It is advisable to share links to your website content regularly on appropriate social media sites. Some platforms such as LinkedIn, provide posting long types of content directly on them.

Social media profiles rank in search engines

Experts suggest that a company is able to rank not only its website but its social profiles as well. By doing this, it will take up valuable real estate at the top of the **search engine result page (SERP)**. This will help a business in defeating competitors in terms of visibility.

For instance, if you type the name of a business in a search engine, its social media profiles will likely pop up along with its official website.

Note: Make sure all appropriate social profiles are active and are consistently engaging with audiences. Also, targeting those platforms that vibrate most with your potential customers is an important to step to proceed with.

Capturing external links is easier with social media

The usage of social media platforms to share and promote your content is the best practice. It increases the likelihood of other websites referring and linking back to it.

The most promising factor in achieving a high page rank is the authority of the websites doing the linking. As per a recent study, this approach works for a longer duration.

Note: Cleverly highlight quality content on social media which people like to connect with. People prefer to link to that content that they want to read and share themselves.

Social media boosts brand awareness

Social media channels, in the last decade, have proven to be well for establishing themselves as generators of brand awareness. The best example is Facebook that has 5.71 billion monthly active users and the number is still increasing month by month. The statistical data shared by Statista illustrates the real picture of social media in boosting brand awareness.

Note: Regular discussions, responding to audience queries, and commenting on news and trends are the best way to engage social audiences.

Local SEO relies on social media

As per a study, it came to notice that 80 percent of smartphone users perform mobile searches to find businesses near them, that is, geography plays a major role in user experience and search engines are paying attention.

For instance, some social websites offer an opportunity to show geographical placement and provide a stage for customers to discuss the business. The success mantra is *"the more people review or engages with your business online, the more likely it is search engines will take notice and incorporate you into local search engine result pages (SERP)."*

Note: Make sure that the geographic information for your business matches across all platforms and websites. Differences in address, phone number, or other information could lead to a lower SERP ranking.

Different search engines are partial to specific social media activity

To explore various activities related to businesses in the social world, various search engines fulfilla promising task for the sake of wider publicity. The purpose of advertising or promotion in the social platform is to attract more and more customers towards the respective brand or product.

The two best examples are Google and Bing. Both search engines do similar kinds of activities. They observe the social control of users, that is, how many users follow them. On the basis of this survey, they assign weight to the respective search engine result pages (SERP).

> **Note: Implement plans in such a manner that you receive as much as possible wide publicity on the social platforms, and hence become eligible for the top page ranker in the SERP listing.**

4.6 Basic concepts: CPC, PPC, CPM, CTR, CPA

Cost per click, pay per click, cost per mill, click through rate, and click per acquisition are the multiple metrics that determine the revenue which the publisher or marketer receives. Here is a brief discussion on them.

CPC: Cost per click

CPC is an internet-based marketing formula used to compute the prices for banner advertisements. In this approach, advertisers pay publishers based on the number of times a banner is clicked. This is a payment method that compensates a publisher whenever their referred customers click on a link for an advertiser's offer.

PPC: Pay per click

In PPC, an advertiser pays an agreed amount per click for advertisements on the publisher sites. For example, Google is the best instance in which the PPC mode of metrics is applicable in which the advertiser utilizes the PPC. So, PPC works similar to CPC but they are termed differently for the publisher and advertiser to be more relevant to what the click actually means and who gets paid or pays.

The bottom line is that you pay for a click on advertisements and the publisher gets paid for the click. In simple terms, **pay per click (PPC)** and **cost per click (CPC)** are one and the same in all honesty in which a publisher will generally utilize a CPC advertising revenue model and get paid for adverts that generate clicks on their website.

> **Note : Do not forget that paying for clicks can also mean that you are getting impressions that cost you nothing, especially with digital display advertising.**

CPM: Cost per milli (thousand)

CPM refers to the number of clicks registered on a website by the readers. For example, AdSense computes advertisement revenue for websites based on CPM. In cost per milli, "m" or 'milli' is the roman symbol for thousand. When these metrics are used in digital advertising, they relate to the cost per thousand-page impressions.

CTR: Click-through rate

CTR is the next valuable metric that helps in measuring the success of an online advertising campaign. A CTR is computed as:

CTR = number of users/the number of times the ad was delivered

Here, CTR is a percentage obtained by dividing the number of users who clicked on an advertisement on a web page by the number of times the advertisement was delivered (impressions).

For instance, if a banner advertisement was delivered 100 times, that is 100 impressions and one person clicked on it, then the resulting CTR would be one percent and would be displayed as 1.00.

CPA: Cost per action or cost per acquisition

In CPA, the publisher takes all the risk of running the advertisement, and the advertiser pays only for the amount of users that complete a transaction such as a purchase or sign up. This is the best type of rate to pay for banner advertisements and the worst type of rate to charge for.

4.7 Importance of landing page

The existence of landing pages is precious for any marketer because it is the platform where you receive conversions or revenue from potential users. Also, it understands and collects prospects, removes distractions, and tracks data in an easy mode.

Generating Leads

There are two main purposes of the website. One is to generate traffic and the second is to convert them into leads. Landing pages help your website in generating leads and convert them into potential customers.

As per a study, it came to be known that marketers capture leads at a higher rate by sending them to dedicated landing pages rather than sending traffic to the home page. The landing page is the most effective way of generating more leads for your sales team.

Collecting prospect demographics

As per experts, it is suggested to collect relevant information based on demographics. It is an alternative medium for extracting information that results in lead generation. Demographics are the method of determining groups of people in a population by their attributes. It is a common practice for businesses to use demographics as the target market.

The potential demographics cover characteristics such as age, gender, marital status, income, education, employment, and so on. Through this characterization, it becomes easier for you to establish the landing page based on user background. Moreover, it will save your effort and time in approaching the target audiences.

Track data

Data tracking is one of the most recommended activities by digital experts for marketers. Data from landing pages help you in understanding the actual status of your prospects. Through the monitoring and analyzing of data, you get an idea of whether prospects are highly engaged or not.

In addition to that, you will retrieve additional information about the prospects' responding behavior. Data tracking signals the approachability of audiences towards your landing page. For example, your shared offers have been downloaded by how many users and in how many number of times.

Remove distractions

It is the natural tendency of any marketer to receive a quick reaction of customers towards their business or landing page. But sometimes, it happens that due to some distractions, there is a delay in customer action. For example, users, instead of reaching your landing page directly, may take a variety of actions like checking your website's about section, profile section, or history section. All such courses of actions take the form of distractions.

To overcome this, a landing page removes all distractions so that your visitors can focus on the one primary thing you want them to do, that is, conversion or sales.

Offer clarity and purpose

Landing pages are short, focused, and are of one page in length. They make it clear to the audiences that you want them to purchase, to contact you, to sign up, or to download. The main objective of the landing page is to convince visitors to take a specific action. It becomes achievable because of the clarity of their approach as you cannot expect them to have to figure out what that is.

Force visitors to make a decision

Most people are uncertain and do not help your business one bit. An effective landing page will force your web visitors to make a decision by eliminating all distractions. It will help them to focus by having a clear message and by having an obvious call to action. This makes you clear about understanding the right client due to the landing page effort in categorizing the segmentation of visitors and non-visitors. In simple terms, you will know once and for all if that web visitor will turn into a lead or not.

Test and optimize

To improve your tasks, testing and optimizing activities should be done on a regular basis. To follow this approach for our betterment, we test and optimize landing pages also. You can test different colors, images, headlines, copies, and form fields to see what is getting people to convert and what is stopping them from doing so. By doing this, you can improve your landing pages based on what visitors respond to the most.

4.8 How to create and test landing pages

The current scenario reflects that internet data is increasing very rapidly. Due to an increase in the number or usage of mobile phones and websites every year, it is   good practice to test your page regularly. It is better to test your landing page for active content and user experience. When your page is lively, the content on your web page by default adapts according to the type of screen being used to access the content by the users.

A/B testing versus multivariate testing

A/B testing is one of the approaches that is used to test landing pages. It is used to compare two versions of a landing page, named 'A' and 'B.' Both landing pages are similar except for one variation that might impact a visitor's behavior. To evaluate the most effective version, web traffic is divided evenly between each version of the page. After the completion of the testing procedure, on the basis of the test result status, the valuable and workable version is considered for follow up.

Multivariate testing, on the other hand, allows you to test various changes found in landing pages altogether. This type of technique is preferred in the situation of in-depth testing. For instance, when there is a requirement of testing various origins within a page, we move ahead with multivariate testing. It performs well to handle heavy web traffic. In simpler terms, it tests different elements within a single web page and is ideal for high traffic websites.

The important themes for testing a landing page include:
- Headline of the page
- Call to action buttons
- Pricing strategies
- Landing page image
- Unique selling proposition
- Sales copy
- Text font and style
- Page layout and design

15 steps for a successful testing campaign:

- Have a clear testing plan.
- Have well-defined, clear, and measurable conversion criteria.
- Identify the important elements to test.
- Use proper testing tools.
- Determine whether A/B or multivariate testing is appropriate.
- Access current traffic and conversion rates.
- Determine target conversion goals.
- Determine number of scenarios to test.
- Determine time span to run tests.
- Create variations of different testing elements.
- Install and deploy different test scenarios.
- Measure test results and findings.
- Do more changes based on findings.
- Conduct follow up tests.
- Track improvements.

Major landing page testing mistakes you should avoid:

- Do not have an effective testing plan.
- Testing with very low traffic.
- Testing too many elements.
- Not establishing the criteria for success.
- Not conducting follow up experiments.
- Not monitoring tests when running.
- Not tracking external factors.
- Running tests for too long.
- Testing small changes and ignoring big concepts.
- Getting caught up in opinions.
- Not measuring the entire funnel.

All the above-mentioned points regarding the successful conduct of tests as well as the mistakes to avoid during testing of landing pages will help you make your website rich, active, and efficient. This effort will result in attracting more and more potential customers towards your business sites.

4.9 User-generated content

User-generated content means any type of digital content that has been created by unpaid members or contributors. By unpaid contribution, it means any user or subscriber of the service that has produced as well as shared the content. This is also known as user-created content.

User-generated content may be defined as being the act of users promoting a brand. It is not produced by the website and its related services. It is the user who plays the role of a follower or fan who puts out the created content on digital platforms like Wikipedia. The type of content includes text, audio, video, images, tweets, blog posts, testimonials, and so on.

User-generated content has a strong historical background. This concept came into existence in the mid-2000s and after that, it arose into the circles of web publishing and the technical content world. For example, the **British Broadcasting Corporation (BBC)** adopted a user-generated content platform for its websites in 2005. Gradually, as web 2.0 platform(s) transformed to web 3.0 platform(s), the usage and popularity of user-generated content also rose in a frequent manner.

4.10 Multimedia video (video streaming)

Multimedia video is regularly shared and presented to an end-user by the publisher. It is one of the preferred mediums for sharing the information on the online platform. Moreover, video streaming is one of the components of multimedia that works well in promotion as well as knowledge sharing. The term "stream" refers to the process of delivering digital media and also refers to the delivery method of multimedia video. It also provides an additional feature of file downloading, a process in which the end-user obtains the entire file for the content before watching or listening to it.

A client end-user can use their digital device to start playing a digital video or audio content before the entire file has been transmitted. The delivery method from the media varies from case to case as most of the delivery systems are either inherently streaming such as radio, television or inherently non-streaming like books and audio compact disks.

Live streaming is the delivery of online content in real-time, much as live television broadcasts content over the airwaves via a television signal. Live internet streaming requires forms of source media such as a video camera, audio interface, and screen capture software. It also includes an encoder to digitize the content, a media publisher, and a content delivery network to distribute and deliver the content. Live streaming does not need to be recorded at the origination point even though it frequently is.

There are challenges with streaming content on the digital platform. If the user does not have enough bandwidth in their internet connection, they may experience stops, lags, or slow buffering of the content. Some users may not be able to stream certain content due to not having compatible computer or software systems.

4.11 Multimedia audio and podcasting

Multimedia audio is a combination of two terms: multimedia and audio. By definition, multimedia is a representation of information in an interactive manner with the use of a combination of text, audio, video, graphics, and animation. For example, **multimedia message service (MMS)**. In multimedia, audio means related to recording. Audio is an important component of multimedia because this component increases the understanding ability and improves the clarity of the concept. The commonly used softwares for playing audio files are QuickTime and RealPlayer.

Multimedia audio is a technology that is used to record, store, manipulate, generate, and reproduce sound using audio signals that have been encoded in digital form. It is a popular medium which makes a revolutionary environment in the digital world. One of the best examples of multimedia audio is a "podcast." This refers to the method of distributing audio files or music videos over the internet. It often refers to both content and method of delivery. It is often used for playback on mobile devices and personal computers.

The "podcast" controls a central list of the files on a server as a web feed. The listener uses a special client application software on a computer or media player which accesses this web feed, checks it for updates, and downloads any new files in the series. This process can be automated to download new files automatically; thus, it may seem to subscribers as though podcasters broadcast. Files are stored locally on the user's device, ready for offline use. Many different mobile applications allow people to subscribe and to listen to podcasts.

Multimedia audio such as podcasts have more than a decade of historical background. The original creator was Ben Hammersley who suggested the word "podcast" as a brand of media player in 2004. The files distributed are in audio format but may sometimes include other file formats such as PDF. Videos shared by following the podcast model are sometimes called video podcasts or video logs.

4.12 Multimedia photos/images

Multimedia photos are the most widely used content in today's scenario. This includes a variety of photos or images and illustrations that are available for usage for the audiences on the digital platforms. Many websites offer multimedia images free of cost. It is easily accessible and reachable for users to grab multimedia images through the online channels. One of the best examples is Shutterstock which is a specialized website for providing multimedia images, stock photos, and so on.

There is also an alternative popular hosting service in the digital world, namely Flickr. It is the platform that hosts images and video services. In this platform, photos and videos can be accessed from Flickr without the need to register an account but an account must be created to upload content to the site. It is beneficial to register an account as it allows users to create a profile page containing photos and videos that the user has uploaded and also grants the ability to add another Flickr user as a contact. It is easily accessible on any device such as a desktop, tablet, laptop, and mobile. For mobile users, Flickr has official mobile apps for iOS and Android, and an optimized mobile site.

Flickr has an appealing historical backdrop. It was developed by Ludicorp in 2004. It has changed ownership several times and has been owned by SmugMug since the second quarter of 2018.

Conclusion

In this chapter, we have discussed the concept of social media marketing and its applicability to various social media channels. We also went through the creation of social media content and its impact on SEO. We discussed the concept of testing the landing pages. Additionally, we highlighted the various multimedia elements used in social media platforms. In the next chapter, we will see an overview of mobile marketing and analytics.

Points to remember

- Social media can also help build links that in turn support SEO efforts. Many people also perform searches in social media sites to find social media content.

- Engaging with prospective clients via social media helps you keep your brand at the top in the minds. By driving social traffic back to official websites, you can increase organic search ranking.

- A/B testing or split testing is an experimental approach for comparing two versions of a landing page, (A and B), which are identical except for one variation that might impact a user's behavior, and to find out the most effective version.

- Multivariate testing enables you to test many changes simultaneously.

MCQs

1. **Social networks are organized primarily around _____.**
   a) Brands
   b) People
   c) Discussions
   d) Interests

2. **What is meant by A/B testing in marketing?**
   a) Testing of two different products
   b) Testing two versions of an advertisement to see which elicits the best response
   c) Clinical testing of medical products before legally allowing them for sale
   d) Testing via two mediums such as radio and television

3. **What is "social media optimization?"**

   a) Creating content which easily creates publicity via social networks

   b) Writing clear content

   c) Creating short content which is easily indexed

   d) Hiring people to create content for social networks

4. **How does creating a social network marketing plan differ from a traditional marketing plan?**

   a) The brand image would be completely different for social marketing

   b) The staff requirements and skillsets for social marketing are different

   c) Other than the method of delivery, a marketing plan, either way, will be similar

   d) None of the above

5. **Which type of marketing would a company blog be considered to be?**

   a) Social network marketing

   b) Traditional marketing

   c) Both

   d) Neither

Answers

1. *b*
2. *b*
3. *a*
4. *b*
5. *a*

Questions

1. What metric do you use to measure the success of your social campaigns?

2. What are social media success tracking tools?

3. What are the marketing strategies to generate leads?

4. What is the most important task of a social media manager?

5. What is the impact of social media marketing on a business?

Key terms

Social media marketing: Social media marketing (SMM) is an approach that focuses on social networks for promoting brand awareness and specific products. It is recognized as a popular type of advertising, and hence, it is assumed to be very effective in building brand awareness.

CHAPTER 5
Mobile Marketing and Web Analytics

Mobile marketing is used to approach potential customers through the multi-channel promotion of products and services. Marketers publicize their brand and goods with the extensive use of mobile gadgets. They reach to the widest range of audiences with varying mobile options such as mobile apps, SMS, e-mail, in-app advertising, quick response (QR) code, and so on. What is the role of mobile marketing in the digital era? What's the use of mobile sites, apps, and widgets? What are web analytic tools and their usages in digital marketing? You will find the answer to these questions in this chapter. So let's get started!

Structure

In this chapter, we will cover the following topics:

5.1   Introduction to mobile marketing

5.2   Overview of B2B and B2C mobile marketing

5.3   Use of mobile sites/web

5.4   Apps (applications) and widgets

5.5   Overview of blogging

Objective

After studying this chapter, you should be able to:

- Understand the importance and usages of mobile marketing.
- Learning the approach of mobile sites.
- Understand the concepts of web analytics and its use case.

5.1 Introduction to mobile marketing

Mobile marketing is one of the best methods to follow in the current scenario of digital marketing. It helps in enhancing the growth of your business in a digital platform. It highlights your brand and products for promotion through mobile features and technology. In the early days, mobile marketing was limited to SMS and MMS but due to technological advancement, it has extended the growth of promotion to another level. In today's digital environment, it includes e-mail, mobile websites, apps, social media, and chat apps. Most of the advanced technologies are less than a decade old which basically reflects how quickly the technology is evolving. In addition to that, we have transformed from mobile phones with a limited set of features to smartphones, a tablet that is capable enough to receive more updates and further share relevant information to wider audiences.

5.2 Overview of B2B and B2C mobile marketing

B2B and B2C mobile marketing explore their individual roles in the form of apps to connect with different domains for business interaction and exploration.

What is a B2B app?

Businesses to business (B2B) apps are frequently used by marketers to establish a connection with other clients or businesses within the company. B2B apps have a different scope of accessibility, that is, some may be accessible to the public whereas others are used privately. The objective of the development of B2B apps is to fulfill a specific requirement like a portal that is used to assign and manage projects, or in-house inventory management.

It is normal to see the usage of B2B apps to provide a marketing tool. For instance, a land surveying company may develop a mobile application to assign site visits to various surveyors so that they can input data into the app. Now, a day's usage of B2B apps becomes marketing trends in the digital world which helps in providing relevant information in an effective and timely manner.

What is a B2C app?

Businesses to consumer (B2C) apps are other well-known apps that are frequently found in places like the app store. They consist of various forms:

- **Loyalty apps:** These are one of the types of B2C apps which are applicable for customer loyalty and rewards-based purpose.
- **E-commerce apps:** These types of B2C apps are preferred for those individuals who create an app uniquely for them. For instance, retailers prefer to create e-commerce apps that contribute specially towards their online shop.
- **Standalone apps:** These forms of B2C apps gain much more publicity in the virtual world. For example, game apps, utility apps, or social apps.

The benefits of B2C apps are that they are capable of exploring themselves in multiple areas but there is one limitation. A major restriction is that they are costlier to implement. B2C apps are dependent on regular users and they require frequent updates in response to user feedback. Also, to measure the success rate and downloads, it is important to regularly maintain the user interface of the apps. To handle the issues, determine user analytics, and to maintain the apps continuously for their proper functioning, a huge expense is required.

5.3 Use of mobile sites/web

The usage of mobile sites/web has increased tremendously in the past decade. Due to the extensive growth of data in the digital world, mobile sites make themselves capable enough in showing their presence as a prime utility. Mobile web refers to browser-based internet services. Through the mobile web, you can access various applications from smartphones or other mobile devices.

The difference between mobile web applications and domestic applications is predicted to be unclear as mobile web applications gain direct access to the hardware of mobile devices. Also, the speed and capabilities of mobile web applications are much better than domestic applications. The demand for domestic applications has reduced due to the preserved storage capacity and accessibility to rigid interface graphic functions.

Due to a huge increase in the number of websites, web 2.0 has been upgraded to web 3.0 which is the revised version of the mobile web. Apart from the enhanced features in the revised version, the mobile web suffers from interactivity and functionality issues even today. Interactivity issues arise from a lack of compatibility in mobile devices, browsers, and mobile operating systems. Functionality issues happen due to limited display resolution and user interface design. In spite of these limitations, the mobile web is being created by mobile developers in many numbers. As per a recent study, it came to notice that the mobile web was found to be the third most widely used platform in the digital world which kept the Android and iPhone operating systems far behind.

5.4 Apps (applications) and widgets

Apps and widgets are the two important pillars of the mobile web. They are considered to be two sides of the same coin. They help us to do the same things; however, their methods are different. Both have their advantages and depending on the app functions and particular needs, you may choose to go with one or the other.

Basics of apps and widgets

Apps are programs that are considered for two categories of apps, namely mobile apps and desktop apps. Apps are developed to perform specific tasks such as mobile apps are developed for small devices such as mobile phones and tablets, whereas desktop apps are developed to run programs locally on a computer system or laptop.

Widgets are more like icons that are linked to a program. They are independent mini-apps that come in all shapes and sizes.

Functions of apps and widgets

The app is a full-highlighted program that has a multifunctional ability to let you do everything at once with ease and comfort. To enjoy the services of the program, you need to tap and open the icon. Unlike apps, widgets are always open by default and you don't need to tap to start the program. Widgets are also apps except that they run in the background.

Hibernating

Closing an app usually leaves its last state and it moves away from its interface. An app hibernates when the instance of that program is terminated. When you open the app again, it reloads its executable file either fully or partially.

On the other hand, widgets are always active in the background so they do not hibernate when you move away from the interface. There is no case of reloading of executable files in the widgets.

Purpose of apps and widgets

When you tap the icon, the app becomes active and it links directs to a third-party program. It needs to be downloaded from the respective online play store before use. The main purpose of an app is to perform a specific task.

Widgets are considered to be a mini version of apps. They are more like an extension of the apps which make the apps easily accessible on the home screen. *Table 5.1* highlights the comparative key points between the app and the widget.

App	Widget
The app is a fully-fledged stand-alone software program specially developed for smartphones.	Widget is an extension of an app that gives access to the frequently used functions of the app.
You need to tap and open the app to start the program.	You need not tap the widget to start the program.
It terminates the instance of the program when moved away from the interface.	It always runs in the background without having to load the instance of the program.
Apps hibernate when the session terminates.	Widgets do not hibernate as they are self-running applications.
Apps need to be downloaded from the respective online store before you can use them.	Widgets came pre-installed with mobile devices.

Table 5.1: Comparison between apps and widgets

Visibility of apps and widgets

An app is visible to the user and it performs its activities in the foreground, however, the instance of that program is closed when you move away from the interface.

A widget is not visible to the user and it runs in the background. It works behind the scenes without having to load the executable files every time when you tap the icon.

5.5 Overview of blogging

A blog is a place to express yourself by sharing your knowledge, thoughts, passions, and viewpoints. You can make it anything you want it to be. Your blog can be an online journal where you just write stories about your life or you can make your blog specific to a single topic. There are blogs about sports, fashion, makeup, travel, parenting, pets, technology, politics, and the list goes on and on.

With passion, time, and effort, you can become a successful blogger. Blogging is easy. Anyone can do it if they put in the time and effort, but not everyone does. In the internet culture, it is widely accepted that only 1% of people on the net are producing content. That leaves the other 99% who are just consuming that content. One thing for sure is that you must have heard that blogging is becoming increasingly popular. However, there is still plenty of room for growth.

So who are those 1% of internet users creating all the content? Some of them are bloggers and they are the kind of people that are brave enough to write about their lives or their passions and share it with the world. They are people just like you and me. Blogging is a universal hobby. From geniuses to the average people, anybody can do it and be successful. It just takes some passion, a little time and effort, and the right guide to get you started.

Some blogs are tremendous; they are basically magazines on the internet. Other blogs are smaller and more personal. Some blogs are just people writing about their lives. Others are focused on one subject in particular. There is a lot of information out there about everything that goes into blogging. But the problem is that it is scattered all over the internet. Good information is hard to find and none of it is complete. Follow along and get the right information in the most convenient manner.

5.6 Introduction to web analytics

Web analytics is the approach that is used to study various patterns and trends that are observed in the online platform. Through web analytic tools, you can gather, measure, report, and analyze web data. It is generally used to analyze web-based data and further optimize its web usage and results. It is also preferred to monitor key metrics, analyze visitor activity, and traffic flow. It is known to be a strategic methodology in gathering data and generating reports.

Importance of web analytics

Web analytics is needed to evaluate the success rate of the website and its linked business. While using web analytics, the following preventive measures can be applied:

- We can identify the problems related to the web content so that they can be rectified in a timely manner.
- Through web analytics assessment, we can have a clear perspective of the various trends of websites.
- Web analytics features help in tracking web traffic data and the corresponding user flow.

- It also gives direction in obtaining the objective of a web analytical study.
- It helps in resolving the challenges to pick potential keywords.
- Web analytics methodology guides in determining the segments for further improvement.
- It escorts in searching the referring sources.

Web analytics process

Web analytics is an ongoing process that helps in attracting more traffic to a site, thereby increasing the return on investment. The primary objective of carrying out web analytics is to optimize the website in order to provide a better user experience. It provides a data-driven report to measure the visitors' flow throughout the website. Take a look at *Figure 5.1*; it shows the process of web analytics.

Figure 5.1: Overview of web analytics process

The six-step process of web analytics is as follows:

1. **Define goals:** It is the initial phase of the web analytics process. It states defining the business goals appropriately

before proceeding to the next step of the process. Work properly on the key findings and objectives. Make sure that you have a clear idea of the process while gaining prerequisite information.

2. **Build KPIs:** The next phase of the web analytics process is to build key performance indicators (KPIs). It is necessary to set KPIs which help in tracking the goal's achievement. KPIs include the time of visit, frequency of visit, duration of visit, and so on.

3. **Collect data:** Data gathering is a sensitive step in the web analytics process. Make sure you collect correct and suitable data. If the data is accurate, then the possibility of achieving the optimized result is high, otherwise inaccurate data will be painful for you in the entire process of web analytics.

4. **Analyze data:** Data analyzing is the intermediate step in web analytics. To extract observations, analyze the data on the basis of received parameters.

5. **Test alternatives:** It is the post step in data analysis. Once the analysis is done, test the alternatives based on the assumptions learned from the data analysis.

6. **Implement:** It is the final step in web analytics which refers to implementing perceptions based on data findings and test reports.

5.7 Types and levels of web analytics

There are three major types and levels in which web analytics perform. These types cover the actual requirements of marketers on the basis of data capture, data reporting, and data analysis. The details are explained in the next section.

Type 1: Data capture

Data capture is one of the levels in web analytics. It focuses on gathering the data as per the need or demand. It includes data capturing for updating or customizing the details of the current or proposed system.

For instance, your expert implements a new tab in your web analytics tools. It works on build-up activity and further links that tab to the admin area. A similar kind of approach is also followed in Google analytics as it helps in properly managing and controlling data at a centralized level. This type of information is shared with the client so that a deep understanding regarding the design is in the knowledge of both the parties, between the client and the expert, for the smooth functioning of the proposed system.

Type 2: Data reporting

Data reporting is the next level in web analytics whose main objective is to provide analytical reports to the clients. As per the requirement, the client contacts the expert for the analytical report on few key points such as how many users visit on a weekly basis, update on bounce rate, and so on. With these key questions, the consultant will generate an analytical report based on existing metrics and hand it over to the client.

Data reporting is an automated approach so it works accordingly, and it does not require much thinking to proceed for the next step in analytics.

Most web analytic tools include some programming packages that are capable of generating data analytical reports in the form of graphs and charts. The graph plotting is done with rich in-built features of data analytical tools which help the client in understanding and analyzing the current status of web activities.

For instance, a deep log analyzer is one of the automated web analytic tools that helps the client generate custom reports from the raw data. It also helps in generating the data report in both HTML and excel format.

Type 3: Data analysis

Data analysis is the approach that helps you in getting a solution to your problem in the form of some analytical study. As a client, you may not know the cause of your current business issue. To determine the return on investment of your business campaign, you can take specific guidance from your advisor or expert.

For example, consider a situation where the client takes guidance from his expert for a key question like "Why are people not watching this page?" In this case, your expert will work on the data analysis which includes the status of the current web page, the content available in web page conveys what type of information, figuring out the metrics related to the web page, and last but not the least, what actions should be taken based on the parameters of the weblog data.

The data analysis report is a text-based report that informs you about the current situation and challenges, and further advises you about the preventive measures you have to follow to overcome the current challenges based on the statistical data highlighted in the report.

5.8 Analytics tools and their use case (Google Analytics and others)

Data analytics tools help businesses analyze the vast amount of data. This data analysis guides marketers to take the relevant decision in their business, and hence gain a competitive advantage. The data analytics software filter the raw data that includes a diverse array of business data from current sales to past records and further transforms into refining the data based on the data scientist query.

Through social media, data analytics optimize the user's buying experience by extracting the weblog data via analytics tools. Through this approach, the user's preferences and likes can be obtained in the form of interesting data. Once the marketer receives the relevant data, it helps them in selling the products to the right audiences. Also, the data analytics application guides them in making differentiation between interestied and non-interested users. In addition, it makes them capable of figuring out the browse to buy conversion via customized offers and packages.

There are various data analytics tools that are easily available for usage purposes. Some of them are open source, that is, freely available and other are paid versions. Apart from these, some analytics tools are also available for the trial version which means for a limited period based on their popularity.

For instance, R, Tableau, Apace Spark, RapidMiner and many more are the best examples of data analytics tools. 'R' programming is the leading analytics tool in the software industry and is widely used for statistics, data modeling, and opinion mining.

Analytics reporting

Data analytics is incomplete without reporting. Analytics reporting gives the necessary understanding to make recommendations based on the data gathering activity through analytics tools. Data is a judgmental element of good decision-making. Good decision-making comes from complete reports, effective analysis, and subsequent implementation. Analytics reporting is capable enough to cover all the critical aspects of judgment-based activities.

The general steps in generating the Google Analytics report are as follows:

1. Sign in to Google Analytics.
2. Navigate to your view.
3. Open reports.
4. Click **Customization > Custom Reports > +New Custom Report.**
5. Enter a title.
6. (Optional) Click **+add report** tab.
7. Select a report type: **Explorer, Flat Table, Map Overlay,** or **Funnel**.
8. Define your dimension and metrics.

5.9 Traffic and behavior report

Traffic and behavior reports provide the complete details regarding behavior flow, site content, landing pages, exit pages, site speed, site search, in-page analytics, and much more.

The in-depth details related to traffic and behavior report are as follows:

1) **Overview**

An overview is one of the most informative sections of traffic and behavior reports. It shows the graphical representation of the volume of traffic that your website actually receives. Other than this, it covers the description of some standards such as:

- **Page view:** Page view is referred to as the essential standard of the overview report. It states that when the user visits the page of your website, then that visit is taken into consideration as a page view. Also, if the user views the page multiple times, then each view is considered as a page view. This number of page view is applicable to the same page as well as different pages of websites.

- **Unique page view:** This criterion is also used in the generation of overview reports. It means that if the frequency of page view by the user is more than once then the initial or first view is measured as a unique page view.

- **Average time on page:** This standard is mostly used for analytical study by marketers. It computes the average time spent by users in viewing a single page or multiple pages.

- **Bounce rate:** The bounce rate is calculated on the basis of the number of times the user left your website without any proceedings. In other words, if the user entered your website and came out of the page through which he/she entered, then it is measured to be a bounce rate.

- **Exit percentage:** The number of users who exit either from a single page or multiple pages of your website is computed in the form of exit percentage.

2) **Behavior flow**

It is necessary to know the exact behavior of users as it helps marketers in taking better decisions for the proper functioning of their business. If we become capable of understanding the interest of potential users, then better product offers and services can be shared with them in an effective manner. To achieve this goal, a report name as behavior flow is generated which calculates the visit of the user path, that is, from the initial page view to the final page view.

3) **Site content**

Site content is the overall description related to the engagement of users to your website. This report includes details of user visits in terms of 'all pages' and 'content drill down' factors.

- **All pages:** It guides you in retrieving information like most visited pages of your website, average time spent on the pages, bounce rate, exit percentage, and page value.

  The page value is determined as:

  Page value = Transaction revenue + Total goal value/Unique page views for single page or set of pages.

- Content drilldown: It helps you by providing a report which consists of information like the top folders of content on your website and the top content within the folder.

4) Landing pages

The landing pages report lets you know the top pages on your website where visitors have visited the most. Metrics for landing page include session details, user's behavior information, and conversion ratio. With these metrics, you can easily identify which pages on your website are most likely to convert visitors into leads.

5) Exit pages

As per advisors, it had been suggested to apply some varying strategies to engage visitors to your website's pages for a longer duration. The probable steps include adding links in the respective page, framing navigation buttons, and providing subscription options. All these inclusions will help with the easygoing of your business in the digital platform and with minimal chances of exit pages.

Exit pages present a report that consist of details like the last page visited by the user before the final exit from the website. This report helps in understanding the behavior of the user.

6) Site speed

The site speed report helps you in analyzing the performance of your website. It is one of the most important concerns of marketers to keep the speed of the site always in the active mode. This report provides graphical representation in terms of the average load time of all pages throughout your website. The various metrics under site speed graphical report are as follows:

- **Average page load time:** This refers to the proportion of duration it takes to load a page from the initiation to the final view.

- **Average redirection time:** This means the average number of moments spent in diverting a page, that is, to a new or different place on the website.

- **Average domain lookup time:** This states the time required by the domain name system (DNS) to search for a page.

- **Average server connection time:** This specifies the average duration spent in establishing a transmission control protocol (TCP) needed for connecting a page.

- **Average server response time:** This mentions the average moment of time your server takes to respond to a user request, including the network time from the user's location to your server.

- **Average page download time:** This discusses the average amount of time required in downloading a page.

For better performance of your website, you can improvise its content and further enhance metrics like page load time, page download time, and other relevant metrics. Alternatively, some effort has to be put in to reduce the size of images, widgets, and plug-ins.

7) **Site search**

Site search fulfills a vital purpose in website enhancement. It provides support in gathering some relevant data in the form of keywords. It is very simple to set up site search metrics on your website.

Keywords are reserved words that have some predefined meanings. A set of keywords help the user a lot to search for information in an effective manner. Moreover, the existence of a website search box not only attracts users to visit your website for a lengthy time but it raises your morale in engaging the users towards your website pages and its related content.

The site search overview report demonstrates the overall metrics for visitors who use the search box on your website. Under these metrics, you can view quick reports for the terms searched, categories, and the pages where visitors initiate a search.

8) **In-page analytics**

The final phase of the traffic and behavior report section is in-page analytics. It lets you view your web pages along with analytical and statistical data. This report provides the overall behavior of your website in consideration of various parameters like the number of site pages visited, hit or file size, most likely or rarely visited pages, the moments of page accessibility, and measure of time spent on a specific page, and so on.

5.10 Evaluate conversions

A good conversion rate is one of the main factors of a successful site or e-commerce business. To make any business activity popular, it is necessary to have a healthy number of conversions. If you want to analyze your status in the marketing field, then the conversion rate is the only medium through which you will get your exact analytics report. To monitor your website and track its success, it is mandatory to determine your conversion rates. Conversion is a digital marketing term that means that users are engaged in your sites. A healthy count of conversion will help you in making your business run in a successful direction.

It is very interesting to know about the varying characteristics of conversions. Some site owners believe that conversion is a customer who finds your online advertisement and buys the product. Their belief is alright but conversion is not limited to this statement. Conversion actually has a wider scope. For example, conversions are also people who read your content and buy your services. In some cases, site owners consider a user watching a video as conversion since a YouTube channel can be a major source of income for site owners.

Before proceeding to conversion tracking in web analytics, first critically think about the type of conversions you want to consider. You can determine your conversions in a manner such as which visitors sign up for e-mail, newsletters, or which visitor produces potential revenue. All the above-highlighted cases are the varying possibilities of conversions. Apart from these, site owners prefer to do conversion tracking for advertisement campaigns. This lets them know which campaigns are producing conversions. Conversion analytics guide site owners in making the decision on whether to pay for cost per click (CPC) advertisements or not.

What is a conversion rate?

You can calculate a conversion rate on the basis of the findings of your site based on the number of activities from your visitors. A conversion rate is an equation that online advertisers and marketers use to compare the total number of visitors to a website to the number that becomes paying users.

Obtaining your conversion rate is a two-step process. You first need to add up your total conversions. This part is dependent on what you consider to be a conversion, and it is important to separate your conversions. For example, you do not want to add up conversions for a newsletter with conversions for a sale. This will change your true revenue numbers.

Add up all your conversion numbers for each activity on your site. Once you have each of your conversion numbers added up, use the following calculation:

*(Total Conversions / Total Visitors to your Site) * 100*

The above calculation gives you a percentage of the total. This percentage tells you the percentage of users who may convert to customers or even potential customers if you use newsletters or videos for selling. You can then work with this rate to determine if your newsletters and sales letters are effective.

Conclusion

In this chapter, we have discussed the concept of mobile marketing and its applicability in the B2B and B2C domains. We went through the usage of mobile sites, apps, and widgets. We also discussed the concept of web analytics and its tools. Additionally, we highlighted the role of conversion rate and its implementation.

Points to remember

- The mobile web, also known as mobile Internet, refers to browser-based internet services accessed from handheld mobile devices, such as smartphones or feature phones, through a mobile or other wireless network.

- Apps are fully-fledged programs that are developed to perform specific tasks and can be categorized into mobile apps and desktop apps. Widgets, on the other hand, are self-contained mini-apps that come in all shapes and sizes. Widgets are more like icons that link to programs.

- Web analytics is the methodological study of online/offline patterns and trends. It is a technique that you can employ to collect, measure, report, and analyze your website data.

- The behavior overview report provides a graph showing the amount of traffic your website receives and additional metrics.

- A conversion rate is an equation that online advertisers and marketers use to compare the total number of visitors on a website to the number that becomes the paying customers, subscribers, or users.

MCQs

1. **Which of the following is a form of mobile marketing?**
   a) Text
   b) Voice call
   c) Graphic
   d) All of the above

2. **Which of the following is the most common delivery channel for mobile marketing?**
   a) Text
   b) Voice call
   c) Graphic
   d) Search engine marketing

3. **What is the full form of LBS in mobile marketing?**
   a) Lead-based service
   b) List-based service
   c) Location-based service
   d) None of the above

4. **What are the key aspects of sending effective push notifications?**

   a) Send highly personalized messages

   b) Send with high frequency

   c) Both A and B

   d) None of the above

5. **What % of mobile web users abandon pages if they don't load within ten seconds?**

   a) 0.60

   b) 0.65

   c) 0.70

   d) 0.75

Answers

1. *d*
2. *a*
3. *c*
4. *a*
5. *b*

Questions

1. What is mobile marketing?
2. How does mobile marketing work?
3. What's the difference between mobile marketing and traditional marketing?
4. What is conversion rate?
5. Discuss various types of web analytics.

Key terms

Mobile marketing: Mobile marketing is one of the best mediums of digital marketing that helps the marketer in promoting their products and services through mobile devices. It reaches targeted audiences and conducts market campaigns with the advanced support of mobile technology.

Bibliography

- Barefoot, Darren and Szabo, Julie (2010) *Friends with benefits: a social media marketing handbook (electronic resource).* 1st ed. San Francisco, CA: No Starch Press.

- Bligh, Philip and Turk, Douglas (2004) *CRM unplugged: releasing CRM's strategic value (electronic resource).* Hoboken, N.J.: Wiley.

- Breitbarth, Wayne (2011) *Power formula for LinkedIn success: kick-start your business, brand & job search.* Austin, Tex: Gazelle [distributor].

- Brian Solis (2010) *Engage!: the complete guide for brands and businesses to build, cultivate, and measure success in the new web (electronic resource).* Hoboken, N.J.: John Wiley & Sons, Inc.

- Buttle, Francis (2009) *Customer relationship management: concepts and technologies (electronic resource).* 2nd ed. Oxford: Butterworth-Heinemann.

- Campbell, C. A., Campbell, M. and Campbell, C. A. (2013) *The new one-page project manager: communicate and manage* any project with a single sheet of paper (electronic resource). Hoboken, N.J.: Wiley. Available at: http://site.ebrary.com/lib/roehampton/Doc?id=10634648.

- Carter, Brian (2011) *The like economy: how businesses make money with Facebook.* Indianapolis, Ind: Que.

- Carter, Brian and Levy, Justin R. (2012) *Facebook marketing: leveraging Facebook's features for your marketing campaigns.* 3rd ed. Indianapolis, Ind: Que.

- Chaffey, D. (2009) *E-business and e-commerce management: strategy, implementation and practice.* 4th ed. Harlow: Financial Times Prentice Hall.

- Chaffey, Dave and Smith, P. R. (2013) *eMarketing excellence: planning and optimizing your digital marketing (electronic resource).* 4th ed. London: Routledge. Available at: https://www.dawsonera.com/guard/protected/dawson.jsp?name=https://dmz-shib-dg-01.dmz.roehampton.ac.uk/idp/shibboleth&dest=http://www.dawsonera.com/depp/reader/protected/external/AbstractView/S9780203082812.

- Chaffey, D., Ellis-Chadwick, F. and Chaffey, D. (2012a) *Digital marketing: strategy, implementation and practice.* 5th ed. Harlow: Pearson.

- Chaffey, D., Ellis-Chadwick, F. and Chaffey, D. (2012b) *Digital marketing: strategy, implementation and practice.* 5th ed. Harlow: Pearson.

- Charlesworth, A. (2014) *Digital marketing: a practical approach (electronic resource).* Second edition. London: Routledge. Available at: http://site.ebrary.com/lib/roehampton/Doc?id=10899392.

- Charlesworth, A. (2015) *An introduction to social media marketing (electronic resource).* London: Routledge. Available at: http://site.ebrary.com/lib/roehampton/Doc?id=10988445.

- Christer Holloman (2012) *The social media MBA: your competitive edge in social media strategy development & delivery (electronic resource).* Chichester: Wiley.

- Clark, Ronald (2008) *Twitter: free social networking for business : 100 success secrets to increase your profits and sales using twitter business strategies (electronic resource).* [Brisbane, Australia: Emereo].

- *Customer loyalty, retention, and customer relationship management (electronic resource)* (2006). Bradford, England: Emerald Group Publishing.

- E-Commerce Times: *E-Business Means Business* (no date). Available at: http://www.ecommercetimes.com/.

- Evans, D. (2012) *Social media marketing: an hour a day (electronic resource).* 2nd ed. Hoboken, N.J.: Wiley. Available at: https://www.dawsonera.com/guard/protected/dawson. jsp?name=https://dmz-shib-dg-01.dmz.roehampton. ac.uk/idp/shibboleth&dest=http://www.dawsonera. com/depp/reader/protected/external/AbstractView/ S9781118227671.

- Gentle, Michael (2002) *The CRM project management handbook: building realistic expectations and managing risk (electronic resource).* London: Kogan Page.

- Goebel, P., Moeller, S. and Pibernik, R. (2012a) 'Paying for convenience', *International Journal of Physical Distribution & Logistics Management,* 42(6), pp. 584–606. doi: 10.1108/09600031211250604.

- Goebel, P., Moeller, S. and Pibernik, R. (2012b) 'Paying for convenience', *International Journal of Physical Distribution & Logistics Management,* 42(6), pp. 584–606. doi: 10.1108/09600031211250604.

- Green, Lelia (2010) *The Internet: an introduction to new media (electronic resource).* Oxford: Berg.

- Hofacker, C. F. (2012) 'On Research Methods in Interactive Marketing', *Journal of Interactive Marketing,* 26(1), pp. 1–3. doi: 10.1016/j.intmar.2011.10.001.

- Holtz, Shel and Demopoulos, Ted (2006) *Blogging for business: everything you need to know and why you should care (electronic resource).* Chicago, IL: Kaplan Pub.

- Jones, S. K. (2009) *Business-to-business Internet marketing: seven proven strategies for increasing profits through internet direct marketing (electronic resource).* 5th ed. Gulf Breeze, FL: Maximum Press. Available at: http://site.ebrary.com/lib/roehampton/Doc?id=10257161.

- Linoff, G. S. and Berry, M. J. A. (2011) *Data mining techniques: for marketing, sales, and customer relationship management (electronic resource).* 3rd ed. Indianapolis, Ind: Wiley Pub., Inc. Available at: http://site.ebrary.com/lib/roehampton/Doc?id=10513818.

- Mathieson, Rick (2010) *The on-demand brand: 10 rules for digital marketing success in an anytime, everywhere world (electronic resource).* New York: American Management Association.

- McGovern, Gerry (2010) *The stranger's long neck: how to deliver what your customers really want online (electronic resource).* London: A & C Black.

- Melanie Mathos and Chad Norman (2012) *101 social media tactics for nonprofits: a field guide (electronic resource).* Hoboken, N.J.: Wiley.

- Moeller, S., Fassnacht, M. and Ettinger, A. (2009) 'Retaining Customers With Shopping Convenience', *Journal of Relationship Marketing,* 8(4), pp. 313–329. doi: 10.1080/15332660903344644.

- Neher, K. (2013) *Visual Social Media Marketing: Harnessing Images, Instagram, Infographics and Pinterest to Grow Your Business Online.* Cincinnati, Ohio: Boot Camp Digital Publishing.

- Newlands, Murray (2011) *Online marketing: a user's manual.* Chichester: John Wiley [distributor].

- Pescher, C., Reichhart, P. and Spann, M. (2014) 'Consumer Decision-making Processes in Mobile Viral Marketing Campaigns', *Journal of Interactive Marketing,* 28(1), pp. 43–54. doi: 10.1016/j.intmar.2013.08.001.

- Peters, K. et al. (2013) 'Social Media Metrics — A Framework and Guidelines for Managing Social Media', *Journal of Interactive Marketing,* 27(4), pp. 281–298. doi: 10.1016/j.intmar.2013.09.007.

- Poynter, Ray (2010) *The handbook of online and social media research: tools and techniques for market researchers.* Chichester: Wiley.

- Rafiq, M., Fulford, H. and Lu, X. (2013a) 'Building customer loyalty in online retailing: The role of relationship quality', *Journal of Marketing Management*, 29(3-4), pp. 494–517. doi: 10.1080/0267257X.2012.737356.

- Rafiq, M., Fulford, H. and Lu, X. (2013b) 'Building customer loyalty in online retailing: The role of relationship quality', *Journal of Marketing Management*, 29(3-4), pp. 494–517. doi: 10.1080/0267257X.2012.737356.

- Rafiq, M., Lu, X. and Fulford, H. (2012a) 'Measuring Internet retail service quality using E-S-QUAL', *Journal of Marketing Management*, 28(9-10), pp. 1159–1173. doi: 10.1080/0267257X.2011.621441.

- Rafiq, M., Lu, X. and Fulford, H. (2012b) 'Measuring Internet retail service quality using E-S-QUAL', *Journal of Marketing Management*, 28(9-10), pp. 1159–1173. doi: 10.1080/0267257X.2011.621441.

- Roberts, M. L. and Zahay, D. L. (2012) *Internet Marketing: integrating online and offline strategies.* Mason, Ohio: South-Western College Publishing; International ed of 3rd revised ed edition (10 April 2012).

- Ryan, D. (2014a) *The best digital marketing campaigns in the world: II (electronic resource).* London: KoganPage. Available at: http://lib.myilibrary.com?id=576966&entityid=https://dmz-shib-dg-01.dmz.roehampton.ac.uk/idp/shibboleth.

- Ryan, D. (2014b) *The best digital marketing campaigns in the world: II (electronic resource).* London: KoganPage. Available at: http://lib.myilibrary.com?id=576966&entityid=https://dmz-shib-dg-01.dmz.roehampton.ac.uk/idp/shibboleth.

- Sheldrake, P. (2011) *The business of influence: reframing marketing and PR for the digital age (electronic resource).* Chichester: John Wiley. Available at: http://site.ebrary.com/lib/roehampton/Doc?id=10510365.

- Smith, P. R. and Zook, Z. (2011) *Marketing communications: integrating offline and online with social media (electronic resource).* 5th ed. London: Kogan Page. Available at: https://www.dawsonera.com/guard/protected/dawson. jsp?name=https://dmz-shib-dg-01.dmz.roehampton. ac.uk/idp/shibboleth&dest=http://www.dawsonera. com/depp/reader/protected/external/AbstractView/ S9780749461942.

- Stephanie Agresta and Bonin B. Bough (2011) *Perspectives on social media marketing: the agency perspective/the brand perspective (electronic resource).* Boston, MA: Course Technology.

- Taken Smith, K. (2012) 'Longitudinal study of digital marketing strategies targeting Millennials', *Journal of Consumer Marketing,* 29(2), pp. 86–92. doi: 10.1108/07363761211206339.

- Tiago, M. T. P. M. B. and Veríssimo, J. M. C. (2014) 'Digital marketing and social media: Why bother?', *Business Horizons,* 57(6), pp. 703–708. doi: 10.1016/j.bushor.2014.07.002.

- Wittkowski, Kristina1 kristina.wittkowski@ebs.eduMoeller, Sabine1 (2011) 'NON-OWNERSHIP PREFERENCE IN BUSINESS-TO-BUSINESS: REASONS FOR LEASING.', *AMA Winter Educators' Conference Proceedings,* 22, pp. 314–314. Available at: http://search.ebscohost.com/login.aspx?d irect=true&db=buh&AN=63696799&site=ehost-live.

- Zhu, F. and Zhang, X. (Michael) (2010) 'Impact of Online Consumer Reviews on Sales: The Moderating Role of Product and Consumer Characteristics', *Journal of Marketing,* 74(2), pp. 133–148. doi: 10.1509/jmkg.74.2.133

Index

Made in the USA
Columbia, SC
22 September 2021